THE CATHOLIC UNIVERSITY OF AMERICA
CANON LAW STUDIES
No. 344

The Obligation of Respect and Obedience of Clerics Toward Their Ordinary

(CANON 127)

A Historical Synopsis and a Canonical Commentary

A DISSERTATION

Submitted to the Faculty of the School of Canon Law of the Catholic University of America in Partial Fulfillment of the Requirements for the Degree of Doctor of Canon Law

by

REVEREND JOSEPH G. SHEEHAN, J.C.L.
Priest of the Diocese of Crookston, Minnesota

THE CATHOLIC UNIVERSITY OF AMERICA PRESS
WASHINGTON, D. C.
1954

NIHIL OBSTAT:
Eduardus G. Roelker, S.T.D., J.C.D.
Censor Deputatus

Washingtonii, die 10 Maii, 1953

IMPRIMATUR:
✠ Franciscus J. Schenk, D.D., J.C.D.
Episcopus Crookstoniensis

Crookstonii, die 15 Maii, 1953

Printed by
MCGARRY PRINTING COMPANY
CROOKSTON, MINNESOTA

To

SAINT JOSEPH

Patron of the Universal Church

TABLE OF CONTENTS

PART II

CANONICAL COMMENTARY

FOREWORD

Unity is one of the four distinguishing marks of the Catholic Church. It is just as characteristic today as it was in the early centuries. This unity includes especially unity of government. Unity of government extends to all members of the Church, laity and clergy alike, because all owe obedience to their respective ecclesiastical superiors in accordance with their various states and positions in the Church. The special obligation of obedience on the part of the clergy flows from the concept of the Church as a juridically perfect society. It should not be surprising, therefore, that the Code of Canon Law incorporates this obligation into its legislation in canon 127: "All clerics, especially priests, are obliged in a special manner to show reverence and obedience to their Ordinary."

The historical synopsis in the first part of this study traces the obligation of clerical obedience from the earliest days of the Church to the present legislation as promulgated in the Code of Canon Law. The canonical commentary in the second part confines itself chiefly to the obligation enjoined upon members of the secular clergy to show reverence and obedience to their Ordinary. Although this duty of clerical obedience expressed in canon 127 extends likewise to the clerical members of Religious Institutes, the writer feels that this aspect has been amply treated in the standard works on the Religious life. The present study concerns itself with clerical members of Religious Institutes only in so far as they are entrusted with positions of administration within the diocese.

The specific object of this work is to point out the principles which determine not only the subjects and objects, but also the basis and extent of the obligation of clerical canonical obedience.

The writer wishes to express his gratitude to the Most

Reverend Francis J. Schenk, D.D., J.C.D., Bishop of the Diocese of Crookston, Minnesota, for the opportunity to pursue graduate studies in Canon Law at the Catholic University of America; to the members of the Faculty of the School of Canon Law for their devoted interest and assistance; and to all relatives and friends who by their material and spiritual assistance have helped to make this work possible.

PART I

HISTORICAL SYNOPSIS

CHAPTER I

LEGISLATION PRIOR TO THE COUNCIL OF TRENT

The concept of the clergy owing respect and obedience to the Bishops and higher ecclesiastical superiors is as old as the Church itself. The early Fathers of the Church made many references to the respect and obedience which is due to the Bishops. [1]

This obligation of obedience on the part of clerics to their Bishops seems to have been taken for granted. The early Fathers seem to give this impression, for in their writings, they rather stress the motives for observing obedience than argue the necessity of this obligation. In the early days of the Church there was no need for formal canonical legislation in this matter, for a cleric who had received Sacred Orders was considered so intimately bound to his spiritual father, the Bishop, that he was expected to fulfill his every command with implicit obedience.[2]

It is safe to say that at no time during this early period of the Church does it appear that a formal written promise of obedience was ever demanded by legislation for the universal Church. Occasionally, as will be seen in the course of this study, there seems to have been a demand for a written promise of obedience on the part of clerics in some particular localities,[3] but at no time did it ever become a practice in the universal Church. There is

(1) St. Ignatius, *Epistola ad Magnesios,* c. XX, — Migne, *Patrologiae Cursus Completus, Series Graeca* (161 vols., Parisiis, 1857-1866), V, 662 (hereafter referred to as *MPG*); *Epistola ad Trallianos,* c. 1, 2—*MPG,* V, 675; *Epistola ad Ephesios,* c. 4,5,6 — *MPG,* V, 647.

Dionysius, *De Ecclesiastica Hierarchia,* c. 1 — *MPG,* III, 370; St. Cyprian, *De Aleatoribus,* c. 2,3,4—Migne, *Patrologiae Cursus Completus, Series Latina* (221 vols., Parisiis, 1844-1864), IV, 287 (hereafter referred to as *MPL*).

(2) Phillips, *Kirchenrecht* (7 vols., Regensburg, 1845-1872) II, 184.

(3) Jaffé, *Regesta Pontificum Romanorum ab condita Ecclesia ad annum post Christum natum MCXCVIII* (2. ed., correctam et auctam auspiciis Gulielmo Wattenbach curaverunt S. Leowenfeld, F. Kaltenbrun-

abundant evidence that clerics in general were obliged to make an oral promise of obedience to their Bishops on the occasion of their ordination.

During the course of history an abuse crept in with this practice, namely, that of exacting fees on the occasion of making this promise of obedience. These fees were known as *munera* and *oblationes.*[4] Once these malpractices were brought into the light, they were reproved and corrected by the decisions of Popes and Councils.[5]

The practice of making this promise of obedience was never forbidden by the decision of any Pope or Council; and moreover, it seems that only one instance occurred in which an apparent suppression of the promise was made by one Council, the Council of Chalon-sur-Saône, held in the year 813.[6]

It is interesting to note that none of the liturgical books,—such as the Leonine, the Gelasian, or the Gregorian Sacramentaries,—contain any reference to a rite by which the *neo-sacerdos* made his promise of obedience to the Bishop.[7]

The *Libri Pontificales* of the eleventh century contained this rite for the most part, but it occurred at the begin-

ner, P. Ewald, 2 vols., Lipsiae, 1885-1888) n. 411 (hereafter referred to as Jaffé); Muratori, *Antiquitates Italicae Medii Aevii* (6 vols., Mediolani, 1738-1743) VI, 371 (hereafter referred to as Muratori).

(4) Muratori, VI, 371.

(5) Paschal II, *Ad Parisiensis Ecclesiae Clericos,* n. 6019; Mansi, *Sacrorum Conciliorum Nova et Amplissima Collectio* (53 vols. in 60, Parisiis, 1901-1927) XX, 1044 (hereafter referred to as Mansi); *MPL,* CLXVIII, 471; also cf. Jaffé, n. 9245; C. 16, X, *de simonia,* V, 3; Jaffé, n. 9669; C. 11, X, *De regulis iuris,* V, 41.

(6) *Concilium Cabillonense* (813), c. 13 — Hardouin, *Acta Conciliorum et Epistolae Decretales ac Constitutiones Summorum Pontificum* (12 vols. Parisiis, 1714-1715) IV, 1034; *Monumenta Germaniae Historica,* Legum Sectio III, *Concilia,* Tomus I, *Concilia Aevi Merovingici, recensuit* Fredericus Maassen, Hannoverae 1883 (hereafter referred to as *MGH*).

(7) Claeys—Bouúaert, *De Canonica Saecularis Obedientia* (Lovanii, 1904), p. 25 (hereafter referred to as Claeys—Bouúaert).

ning of the ordination ceremony, not after the Communion of the Mass, where it occurs today.[8]

However, the Roman Pontifical, in a definitive edition in 1485, preserved the promise of obedience to be made by the newly ordained priest placing his hands between the hands of the ordaining Bishop. Finally, Pope Clement VIII, by the Bull *"Ex quo in Ecclesia"* on February 10, 1596, extended this rite to the Universal Church as obligatory.[9]

The formula of the promise of obedience which a newly ordained priest makes today to the ordaining Bishop is very similar to the one described in the *Libri Pontificales* of the eleventh century. The formula as it is contained in the ordination ceremony today reads, "Promittis mihi et successoribus meis reverentiam et obedientiam?" to which the newly ordained priest replies, "Promitto." [10]

The origin of, or occasion for, demanding the promise of obedience seems to trace to the element of sheer necessity. The ecclesiastical superiors had to make certain that their subjects would adhere to them in the face of schisms and dissensions, which were threatening the unity of the Church. Strange as it may seem, the first instance

(8) "Tametsi in antiquioribus Pontificalibus libris, ritus ipse minime appareat, ut post Communionem proprio Episcopo ordinati Presbyteri promitterent obedientiam; reperitur tamen in plerisque . . . non quidem in fine Missae, sed initio Ordinationis, Episcopo Ordinandum interrogante hoc modo, "Vis Episcopo tuo, ad cuius parochiam ordinandus es obediens et consentiens esse secundum iustitiam et ministerium tuum?" Cui ille respondebat "Volo" — Catalanus, *Pontificale Romanum,* (3 vols., Parisiis, 1850) I, De ordinatione presbyteri, p. 289; Martène, *De Antiquis Ecclesiae Ritibus* (4 vols., 2. ed., Antverpii, 1736-1737), Lib. I, cap. VIII, art. IX, n. 21 (hereafter referred to as Martène).

(9) *Codicis Iuris Canonici* Fontes, cura Emi Petri Card. Gasparri editi (9 vols., Romae: Typis Polyglottis Vaticanis, 1923-1939. Vols. VII-IX, ed. cura et studio Emi Iustiniani Card. Serédi), n. 180 (hereafter referred to as *Fontes*); Claeys-Bouúaert, p. 27.

(10) *Pontificale Romanum, Summorum Pontificum iussu editum, a Benedicto XIV et Leone XIII, Pontificibus Maximis, recognitum et castigatum* (Mechliniae, 1895), Tit. *De ordinatione presbyteri.*

of a promise of obedience as extant today is that exacted by the anti-pope Novatian in approximately the year 251. With this promise of obedience, Novatian endeavored to impede the return of his adherents to the communion of Pope Cornelius. A few weeks after the election of Pope Cornelius (251-253), Novatian, a Roman priest, established himself as anti-pope and threw the whole Christian world into confusion. Pope Cornelius wrote Fabius, the Bishop of Antioch, three letters in which he pointed out in detail the faults in Novatian's election and conduct. (11) In one of these letters, Pope Cornelius brought to Fabius' attention the fact that Novatian made his adherents swear by the Body and Blood of Christ that they would never desert him, or return to Cornelius. (12)

Article 1. Relationship between Bishop and Ordinand Prior to the Fourth Century

There seems to be no vestige of any general or particular legislation or practice by which clerics were bound to their Ordinary by a formal pledge or written promise of obedience in the first three centuries of the Church. This is not surprising, for clerics were by the very fact of their ordination considered as united to their Bishop in a bond so intimate that it could not be dissolved except with the greatest difficulty.(13) Since this bond was so firm and the obligations arising therefrom were so evident, it seemed superfluous to endeavor to strengthen it with pledges and promises.(14) This seems to have been

(11) Chapman, "Cornelius,"—*The Catholic Encyclopedia* IV, 375; Chapman, "Novatian and Novatianism,"—*The Catholic Encyclopedia* XI, 138.

(12) Mansi, I, 827; *MPL,* III, 756; Jaffé, n. 106.

(13) Thomassinus, *Vetus et Nova Ecclesiae Disciplina circa Beneficia et Beneficiarios* (10 vols., Moguntiaci, 1787), Pars II, lib. II, cap. XLIV, n. 1 (hereafter referred to as Thomassinus); Hallier, *De Sacris Electionibus et Ordinationibus* (2. ed., 3 vols., Romae, 1740), Vol. I, p. 213, Pars I, sec. 6, n. 12.

(14) Phillips, *Kirchenrecht,* Vol. II, p. 184; Claeys-Bouúaert, p. 21

the accepted interpretation, since Thomassinus has concluded that up to the year 450 it was unheard that such a promise of obedience be demanded or given in writing.[15]

This opinion seems to have been based on a letter of Pope Leo the Great (440-461) to Anastasius of Thessalonica and Primate of Macedonia. Though this case, strictly speaking, was not concerned with the promise of a cleric to his Ordinary but with a cleric of a higher order (Archbishop) in relation to his Primate; yet since it serves as the basis for future legislation and interpretation, it is inserted at this point.

When Anastasius made Atticus the Metropolitan of Epirus, he demanded from Atticus a promise of obedience in writing. Although Atticus was the Archbishop of Epirus, nevertheless he had to tender obedience to the Primate of Macedonia, namely the Archbishop of Thessalonica.[16] Pope Leo reminded Anastasius in rather strong terms that this abuse of power would not be tolerated, and that no promise of obedience in writing was to be demanded, since this had already been intimated by Atticus' accepting the office.[17]

It may be concluded, therefore, that up to the pontificate of Pope Leo the Great (440-461), promises exacted in writing were not countenanced, and that nothing more was demanded than a promise to become more conversant with one's faith and to observe the canons of the Church.[18]

(15) Thomassinus, Pars II, lib. II, cap. XLIV, n. 1.

(16) Gonzallez-Tellez, *Commentaria Perpetua in Singulos Textus Quinque Liborum Decretalium Gregorii IX* (5 vols., Lugduni, 1673), Lib. I, tit. XXXIII, n. 3 (hereafter referred to as *Commentaria*).

(17) Leo Episcopus urbis Romae, Anastasio Episcopo Thessalonicensi, anno 446;

"Legebatur in litteris tuis, quod frater Atticus chartulam de obedientiae sponsione conscripserat, in qua signum injuriae prodebatur. Non enim fuerat necessarium, ut obligaretur scripto qui obedientiam suam jam voluntarii adventus officio comprobabat"—Jaffé, n. 411; c. 3, X, *de majoritate et obedientia*, I, 33.

(18) Thomassinus, Pars II, lib. II, cap. XLIV, n. 1.

Article 2. Conciliar Legislation in the East

Section 1. Legislation in the Council of Antioch (341)

The first mention in conciliar law concerning the obligation of canonical obedience on the part of clerics to their Ordinaries is found in the legislation of the Council of Antioch, held approximately in the year 341.

Canon 3 of this Council stated that if any cleric should leave his *"paroecia"* (territory or diocese) and migrate to another and remain there for a long time, he should no longer be allowed to officiate, especially if his own Bishop had summoned and urged him to return to his own territory or diocese. If he should persist in his disobedience and not return, he should be wholly deposed from his ministry and be given no opportunity of restoration. And if another Bishop should receive such a deposed cleric, he, in turn, should be punished by the common synod as one who nullifies ecclesiastical law.[19]

Section 2. Legislation in the Council of Chalcedon (451)

The next mention in conciliar law concerning the obligation of canonical obedience on the part of clerics to their Ordinaries is found in the legislation of the Council of Chalcedon, held in the year 451. Canon 8 of this

[19] "Si quis presbyter, aut diaconus, et omnino quilibet ex clero, parochiam propriam deferens, ad aliam properavit, vel omnino demigrans, in alia parochia per multa tempora nititur immorari, ulterius ibidem non ministret, maxime si suo episcopo, et regredi ad propriam parochiam commonenti, obedire contempserit. Quod si in hac indisciplinatione perdurat, a ministerio modis omnibus removeatur, ita ut nequaquam locum restitutionis inveniat. Si vero pro hac causa damnatum alter episcopus suscipiat, hic etiam a communi synodi coarguatur tanquam ecclesiastica jura dissolvens." Bruns, *Canones Apostolorum et Conciliorum Saeculorum IV-VII* (2 vols., Berolini, 1839) I, 81 (hereafter referred to as Bruns); Hardouin, I, 593; Mansi, II, 1330.

Council made it quite clear that clerics who were placed over almshouses, monasteries, or shrines of the martyrs remained under the power (jurisdiction) of the Bishop.[20] It is significant to note that this obligation of obedience to the Bishop was not considered an innovation, but rather that it was considered to be the practice previous to this legislation. This is apparent through the use of the words *secundum patrum traditiones.* The clerics referred to in this canon were the ones entrusted with the spiritual ministrations of houses established for the care of the poor and the sick, and of monasteries and oratories. Following the traditions of the Fathers, the Council rejected any claim on the part of such clerics to exemption from the jurisdiction of their Ordinaries. The Bishop was the administrator of Church property and the director of poor-relief. The responsibility of the Bishop in this matter was inherent in the nature of his office, and it was but natural that the ones appointed by him to attend to the administration of the spiritual and temporal needs of charitable institutions should be subject to his jurisdiction.[21] The penal sanctions levelled against those who had charge of these institutions, in the event that they presumed to withdraw from the jurisdiction of the Bishop were quite strong, viz., if they were clerics, they were to be punished by censures (corrections according to the canons); and if they were lay people or monks, they were to be excommunicated. Monks were at that time not considered as belonging to the clergy, but rather to the laity.

(20) "Clerici . . . sub episcoporum . . . secundum sanctorum patrum traditiones, potestate maneant, nec per contumaciam ab episcopo dissiliant. Qui vero audent evertere huiusmodi formam quoquo modo, nec proprio subjacebunt; si quidem laici vel monachi fuerint, communione priventur." Mansi, VII, 375.

(21) Schroeder, *Disciplinary Decrees of the General Councils* (St. Louis: Herder, 1937), p. 97.

Article 3. Conciliar Legislation in the West

Section 1. Practice of the Church in Spain

a) IV Council of Toledo (633)

In the course of the seventh century there occurred a notable example of particular legislation in the Church of Spain relative to canonical obedience. In the IV Council of Toledo, held in the year 633, it was stated in canon 27 that all priests and deacons stationed in parishes throughout the diocese were to make a profession to the Bishop to practice celibacy and to observe the canons.(22)

The term parish began to be applied to rural congregations in the fourth century, and by the sixth century had come into common, though not exclusive, use in designation of them, for the term still continued to be used for some time in designation of a diocese as well.(23)

b) XI Council of Toledo (675)

In another national Council held at Toledo in the year 675, after a recapitulation of the foregoing legislation, there was an indication that no one was to be promoted to ecclesiastical positions unless, prior to his ordination, he had made a solemn profession of the Catholic Faith and a promise to practice obedience and to observe the canonical laws and mandates of his prelate (Bishop). Besides the confession of faith and the general promise to observe the canons legislated in the IV Council of Toledo (633), there was added the express legislation that a promise of obedience to the Bishop be demanded

(22) "Quando presbyteri vel diaconi per parrochias constituuntur oportet eos professionem episcopo facere . . . " Bruns, I, 231.

(23) "Coeptum est saeculo circiter quarto, sed nonnisi saeculo sexto eiusmodi ruralibus a pagis ecclesiis nomen paroeciae factum est commune." De Luca, *Theatrum Veritatis et Justitiae* (Coloniae Agrippinae, 1706) I, *De Beneficiis*, n. 306.

of all who were aspiring to ecclesiastical positions.[24] This legislation, according to Schneider, was introduced into the canons of this Council to impress the clergy with the gravity of the promise.[25]

Section 2. Practice of the Church in Italy

From an examination of witnesses concerning a dispute between the Bishops of Arezzo and Siena in the year 715 one can deduce that a similar practice of demanding a promise of obedience from clerics prior to their ordination flourished in Italy in the early part of the eighth century.[26] For when interrogated, the witnesses (priests and deacons) refused to testify against their Bishop, since they had given their promise of obedience according to the custom, at the time of their ordination. At least twenty priests and deacons offered their testimony, and the majority of them in their responses made mention of the obedience which they had made at the time of their ordination. For brevity's sake, three examples will be given here in order that the reader may have a better idea of the state of mind of the clerics at that time. Semeris, a priest of the monastery of St. Ampfianus, was the first witness to testify . . . *sacramentum secundum consuetudinem idem* (Aretine) *prebui.* Gunther, a priest

(24) Canon 10: " . . . Et ideo placuit huic sancto concilio, ut unusquisque qui ad ecclesiasticos gradus est accessurus non ante honoris consecrationem accipiat, quam placiti sui innodatione promittat, ut fidem catholicam sincera cordis devotione custodiens, juste et pie vivere debeat, et ut in nullis operibus suis, canonicis regulis contradicat; atque ut debitum per omnia honorem, atque obsequii reverentiam praeeminenti sibi unusquisque dependat . . . " c. 6, D, XXIII.

(25) " . . . das mehr gefürchtet und gehalten wird, was speciell versprochen wird, als was blos einem allgemeinen Versprechen enthalten ist." Schneider, "Der Kanonische Gehorsam,"—*Archiv für katholisches Kirchenrecht* (Innsbruck, 1857-1861; Mainz, 1862-), LXXXII (1902), 294.

(26) Muratori, VI, 371.

of the church and baptistry of St. Stephen, Acennano, testified thus . . . *et salutationes et obedientiam idem habui* . . . [27] The fourth priest to be interrogated replied thus . . . *obedientiam secundum canones idem habui usque modo; et sacramentum ad Sanctum Donatum prebui, et manu mea scripsi* . . . It is interesting to observe that the testimony of the fourth witness referred to his promise of obedience as having been given in writing.

It is quite evident that all these priests and deacons were very conscious of their obligation of obedience to the Bishop. [28]

An example of the profession of obedience which Urispertus, a cleric of Lombardy, made to Peredeus, Bishop of Lucca, in the year 772, offers the following information, namely, that this promise of obedience was given in writing *(chartulam)*, that he promised to donate annually two good sheep (berbices bonos) to the Bishop and his successors, and that if the foregoing provisions were not fulfilled by him, he would make a payment of fifty solidi of gold. The formula is herewith given in its principal parts:

> Urispertus Clericus Peredeo Lucensi Episcopo pollicetur rectum regimen Ecclesiae Sancti Cassiani de Controne. Anno 772
>
> In nomine Dei . . . Modo vero per hanc chartulam repromittere prevideo ego, qui supra, Urispertus Clericus, tibi venerabili Domino meo Peredeo, in Dei Nomine Episcopo, ut in omnibus obediens tibi secundum Sanctos Canones esse debeam, simul et Successoribus sicut alii Sacerdotes vestri. . . Et per singulos annos vobis et successoribus vestris reddere promitto duos berbices bonos in Natale Gerbasi his Luca. . . . Et si haec omnia superscripta capitula a me adimpleta et conservata non fuerint, spondeo ego, qui supra Urispertus Clericus tibi Domno meo Peredeo in Dei Nomine Episcopo

(27) The term *sacramentum* refers to the promise of obedience. c.f. Thomassinus, Pars, II, lib. II, cap, XLV, n. 2. Muratori informs us that these *salutationes* were free-will offerings "salutationes, spontaneas nempe oblationes"—Muratori, VI, 371.

(28) Muratori, VI, 371.

et Successoribus tuis componere auri soledos numero quinquaginta. Et pro confirmatione Rachiprandum Clericum scribere rogavi. Actum Luca

Signum Manus Urisperti Clerici qui hanc Chartulam fieri rogavit.

Dd. Signum [29]

Section 3. Practice of the Church in the Frankish Kingdom

a) Council of Agde (506)

The first canonical legislation found in the Frankish Kingdom is that of the Council of Agde, in South Gaul, near the shore of the Mediterranean Sea, in the province of Languedoc, held in the year 506. Canon eight of this Council stated that if a cleric leaves his office and has recourse to a secular judge to escape ecclesiastical punishment, then he and the judge who admits him shall be excommunicated.[30] While this canon did not specifically mention the obligation of canonical obedience it certainly implied it.

b) Council of Mainz (813)

In canon ten of the Council of Mainz, held in the year 813, the general principle was laid down that clerics are to show proper obedience to their ecclesiastical superiors.[31]

(29) Muratori, VI, 412.

(30) ". . . clericus si relicto officio suo propter districtionem, ad saecularem judicem confugerit, et solatium ei defensionis impenderit, cum eodem de ecclesiae communione pellatur." Bruns, II, 147; Mansi, VIII, 325; Hardouin, II, 999; it was later quoted by Gratian, c. 1, C. XXI, q. 5.

(31) "Discretionem . . . senioribus quoque debitam obedientiam, neque ullo jactantiae studio se attollant . . ." *MGH,* Legum Sectio III, *Concilia*

c) II Council of Chalon-sur-Saône (813)

If one considers the legislation of the early ninth century of the Church in the Frankish Kingdom, it would seem at first glance that this practice of demanding a promise of obedience was rejected. Thus canon 13 of the II Council of Chalon-sur-Saône (813) would give one this impression. Since so much depends upon the interpretation of this canon, rather than attempt to translate it, the writer will set it down in its full original form.

> "Dictum est interea de quibusdam fratribus, quod eos quos ordinaturi sunt jurare cogant, quod digni sint et contra canones non sint facturi, et obedientes sint episcopo qui eos ordinant et ecclesiae in qua ordinantur, quod juramentum, quia periculosum est, omnes una inhibendum statuimus." [32]

Bishops began to force all who were to receive Sacred Orders to swear that they were worthy and to make a profession to comply faithfully with the rules of the canons and to be obedient to the Bishop.

There is a divergence of opinion with respect to this particular legislation. Some were of the opinion that the very practice of exacting this promise was absolutely forbidden. Such seems to have been the mind of Thomassinus (1619-1695), who maintained that the demanding of this promise or oath of obedience was forbidden, because this practice was not in conformity with the Gospel, which forbids all unnecessary oaths.[33] Another who held to his opinion was Richter (1808-1864), who maintained that this practice of the Bishops in demanding a promise

Aevi Karolini, Pars I, p. 263; Hartzheim, *Concilia Germaniae* (11 vols., Coloniae Augustae Agrippensium, 1759-1790) I, 407. This was later incorporated in the *Decree of Gratian*, c. 3, D. XXIII.

(32) Hardouin, IV, 1034; Mansi, XIV, 95.

(33) ". . . hanc jurandi novitatem damnavit synodus; cum juramenta omnia minus necessaria evangelicis litteris proscribantur."—Thomassinus, Pars II, lib. II, cap. XLV, n. 1.

of obedience was expressly disapproved.[34] Scherer (1845-1918) likewise maintained that this practice of demanding an oath on the occasion of ordination was forbidden as being contrary to the canons and a dangerous novelty. Speaking of this canon of the II Council of Chalon-sur-Saône, he made the following observation; "*. . . gegen einen von den Ordinanden zu verlangenden Gehorsamseid als eine uncanonische und gefährliche Neuerung.*" [35]

Others held that by this particular canon, not the actual practice of demanding a promise of obedience was forbidden, but rather the abuse which in the course of time had intruded. The latter was the object of this condemnation. Thus Hinschius (1835-1898) offered the observation that the prohibition should not be taken out of its context and that the promise was not forbidden as such, but as it was described by the Council. It is not to be concluded from the words, *quod digni sint,* that these professions were suppressed, for, according to Hinschius, they signified nothing more than that those who professed them should be free from all irregularities against the canons.[36]

Schulte, (1827-1914) in reference to this canon of the Council of Chalon-sur-Saone and in connection with the legislation contained in the Capitulary of Louis the Pious, (817) which will be taken into consideration shortly, made the bald statement that neither the Council of Chalon-sur-

(34) "Dieselbe Vorschrift findet sich sowohl für die Bischöfe als die niederen Geistlichen auch in Frankenreiche wiewohl hier eine eidliche Verpflichtung ausdrücklich gemissbilligt wurde."—Richter-Dove, (8. ed., 2 vols., Leipzig, 1886) Vol. I, p. 472, n. 145.

(35) Scherer, *Handbuch des Kirchenrechts* (2 vols., Graz., 1886-1898) Vol. I, p. 445, n. 57.

(36) "Auch hier handelt es sich offenbar nur um das Verbot eines Eides in der gedachten Fassung, namentlich soweit der Geistliche danach selbst seine Würdigkeit zu beschwören hatte, nicht um das eines Gehorsameides überhaupt."—Hinschius, *Das Kirchenrecht der Katholiken und Protestanten in Deutschland* (6 vols., Berlin, 1869-1897), Vol. III, p. 210, n. 5.

Saône nor the Capitulary of Louis implied a prohibition of the promise of obedience.[37]

Claeys-Bouúaert maintained the opinion that this legislation was directed against the concomitant abuses rather than against the actual practice of demanding the promise of obedience.[38]

d) Capitulary of Louis the Pious (817)

Similarly no general condemnation of these promises can be drawn from the prohibition contained in the Capitulary of Louis the Pious (817), cap. 16. Because of the importance of this legislation the entire canon will be given. It stated:

> "De episcopis vero in Langobardia constitutis, qui ab his quos ordinabant, sacramenta et munera contra divinam et canonicam auctoritatem accipere vel exigere soliti erant, modis omnibus inhibitum est, ne ulterius fiat." [39]

The legislation of the Capitulary of Louis the Pious is very forceful, but another element enters the picture here, for along with these promises *(sacramenta)* were joined offerings *(munera)*. Hence one is led to suspect that the demand of these gifts and offerings led to abuses, and that these were the object of the condemnation.[40]

Another indication that the promise of obedience was not absolutely forbidden, is apparent from the account of the deposition of Hincmar, Bishop of Laon. In the year 871, at the Council of Ardennes (Douzy), testimony

(37) "Conc. Cabillon. II und Aquisgr. a. 817 c. 16 enthalten kein Verbot des eidlichen Gelöbnisses."—Schulte, *System des allgemeinen katholischen Kirchenrechts* (Giessen, 1856), p. 289, n. 4.

(38) Claeys-Bouúaert, p. 24.

(39) *MGH,* Legum Sectio II, Tomus I, *Capitularia Regum Francorum,* (denuo edidit Alfredus Boretius, Hannoverae, 1883), 278; Hartzheim, I, 546.

(40) Thomassinus, Pars II, lib. II, cap. XLV, n. 2.

was given which brought out the fact that Hincmar not only had made a promise of obedience to the Metropolitan of Rheims, but also the fact that he had made a *written* promise.[41]

The Council of Rouen, held in the year 1074, offers another indication that this profession of obedience was not entirely forbidden, as may be gathered from canon 5 of this Council. This fifth canon stated that sub-deacons, deacons, and parish priests should not be ordained unless they had made the profession prescribed by the Council of Toledo, in the presence of the Bishop. This profession, as was pointed out earlier in this work, was that of canonical obedience to the Bishop.[42]

Scholion 1. Promise of Obedience Prescribed for Special Positions

Vestiges of this oath of canonical obedience on the part of Abbots and Canons to the Bishop of the diocese can be found in the eleventh century. Thus in a letter of Fulbert, Bishop of Chartres, to his fellow Bishop, Fulonus, one reads that a certain Benedictine abbot had slighted Fulonus, and was unmindful of the promise of obedience which was due him canonically. This letter was dated *circa* 1008.[43]

A faint reference in regard to the promise which Canons were required to make can be found in a letter of Gregory

(41) "Et non debuerat oblivisci professionis et subscriptionis suae, ante ordinationem episcopalem; qui coram altari S. Mariae, et cunctis qui adfuerunt, non solum de Rhemensi ecclesia, et de Landunensi parochia, verum et de Rhemorum provincia episcopis, et aliis diversi ordinis viris, secundum morem Rhemensis ecclesiae, sicut soliti erant episcopi ordinandi subscribere, post catholicae fidei professionem, de obedientia sua secundum sacras regulas erga Rhemorum metropolitanum manu subscripsit." Cap. IX. Mansi, XVI, 589.

(42) Hardouin, VI, 1519; also cf. *supra* p. 8.

(43) Fratri et Coepiscopo suo Fuloni, Fulbertus Carnotensium Episcopus,

VII (1073-1085) to the Canons at Le Puy-en-Velay, which is approximately thirty miles southwest of Lyons, France. This letter was written about the year 1077.[44]

Scholion 2. Supression of Malpractices Connected with Promise of Obedience

The malpractice of demanding fees on the occasion of ordinations of clerics, when the promise of obedience was made, as well as on the conferral of benefices, became quite widespread, and several Popes took steps to put an end to this sad state of affairs.[45] Pope Paschal II (1099-1118) likewise made an effort to curb these abuses. On April 6, 1105, he dispatched a letter to the clergy of Paris, in which he forbade the *majores praebendarii* to receive *homagia from the minores praebendarii.*[46] The *homagia* spoken of in this letter of Pope Paschal included not only a promise of obedience, but also some temporal servitude.[47]

"Quod ad praesens . . . Igitur si abbas sancti Benedicti de vestro contemptu culpam suam recognoverit, et illam deinceps subjectionem promiserit quae vobis canonice debetur . . . ut ipsam quoque subjectionem canonicam vobis derogare contendit. . . ." Ep. XVII (c. 1008): *MPL,* CXLI, 208.

(44) Gregorius VII, *Epistola ad Canonicos Anicensis* (c. 1077):
"Notum est vobis qualiter Stephanus Anicensis Ecclesiae invasor et simoniacus, despecto sacramento quod nobis super corpus sancti Petri . . . non cessat."—*MPL,* CXLVIII, 471; Jaffé, n. 5028.

(45) "Cum saeculis XI et XII mos invaluisset multiplicandi sacramenta fidei seu hominia quae vassali dominis temporalibus exsolvebant, etiam abusus aliquando irrepserit, quo majores praebendarii a minoribus talia hominia exigerent."—Thomassinus, Pars II, lib. II, cap. XLVI, n. 7; Claeys-Bouúaert, p. 26.

(46) Mansi, XX, 1044; Jaffé, n. 6019.

(47) "Etsi homagium ac fidelitas promiscue aliquando usurpentur, diversa tamen sunt; nam homagium est promissio obsequii, et servitii temporalis; fidelitas vero praestatur, cum quis promittat superiori servare reverentiam et fidelitatem a jure debitam." Gonzalles-Tellez, *Commentaria,* ad c. 16, *de simonia,* V. tit. III, n. 4.

Article 4. Gratian and the Decretists (1139-1159)

In Distinction XXIII of his *Decretum*, Gratian treated the various ecclesiastical offices, beginning with the highest and descending to the lowest. In the third chapter of this Distinction he treated of the manner of life clerics were expected to lead. After enumerating a long list of counsels and prohibitions, he mentioned that clerics are to show a proper obedience to their elders.[48]

Guido de Baiso (+1313) pointed out that by the word "elders" *(senioribus)* was to be understood "prelates" *(praelatis)*.[49]

Gratian in this particular passage was repeating more or less verbatim the particular legislation of canon 10 of the Council of Mainz, held in the year 813.[50]

In chapter six of the same Distinction, Gratian reiterated the legislation of the XI Council of Toledo (675), which stated that any cleric who was to be promoted to higher orders had to promise to obey the canonical regulations and show reverence to his superior.[51]

Rufinus (+1190) stated that this promise *(placitum or pactum)* referred to an act of the cleric's free-will, whereby he gave his word that he would guard the Catholic Faith with a sincere and devoted heart, that he would live justly and piously, that by none of his actions would he conduct himself in a manner contrary to the rules of the canons, and that likewise in all things he would show due honor and obedience to his prelate, upon whom he depended.[52]

(48) "His igitur lege Patrum cavetur ut . . . senioribus quoque debitam praebeant obedientiam, neque ullo iactantiae studio semetipsos attollant . . ."—c. 3, D. XXIII.

(49) *Rosarium, seu in Decretalium Volumen Commentaria* (Venetiis, 1577), ad c. D. XXIII.

(50) Hartzheim, I, 407-408.

(51) Cf. *supra*, p. 8.

(52) *Summa Decretorum* (ed. Heinrich Singer, Paderborn, 1902), p. 53

Guido de Baiso stated that this promise was to be committed to writing, so that, if later the cleric wished to challenge the promise he had made, he would be confronted by his own promise in writing.[53] He maintained, however, that this promise *(placitum or pactum)* referred to a promise to observe continence, but he did not offer any argument to sustain this opinion.[54]

The next piece of legislation in Gratian's *Decree* is taken from the third canon of the Council of Antioch, held in the year 341. According to this legislation a cleric should not be excommunicated or deprived of his office unless he had first received a warning or an admonition. The legislation provided for the case in which a cleric upon his own authority left the church to which he had been assigned by his own proper Bishop. In this event, if the cleric did not return after having been admonished by his Bishop, he was to be suspended; and if he remained contumacious, he was to be deposed, without any hope of reinstatement. Likewise he was not to be accepted by any other Bishop. If another Bishop nevertheless accepted such a deposed cleric, he became liable for a reprimand in the Synod for weakening ecclesiastical discipline.[55]

The following legislation is taken from a letter attributed to Pope Pius I, (140-155) *"Scitis fratres quia."* But this letter is rather a spurious product of the collection of the false decretals dating from the year 852.[56] In this passage, Gratian proposed three cases dealing with the *privilegium fori.*[57] If a priest or any other cleric was disobedient to his Bishop, or tried to entrap him, or

[53] "Haec enim promissio est in scriptis redigenda, ut si postea velit aliud facere, obviet sibi propria scriptura."—Guido de Baiso, *op. cit.*, p. 30.

[54] *Loc. cit.*

[55] C. 24, C. VII, q. 1. Cf. Bruns, I, 81; Hardouin, I, 593; Mansi, II, 1330.

[56] Jaffé, n. 48; Cf. Hinschius, *Decretales Pseudo-Isidorianae et Capitula Angilrammi* (Lipsiae, 1863), p. 118.

[57] C. 18, C. XI, q. 1.

insulted or calumniated or reproached the Bishop, he was to be turned over to the civil court, deposed, and punished accordingly.[58] The reason given in the *Ordinary Gloss* was that such a cleric had become incorrigible.[59] Rufinus pointed to the same reason for this punishment.[60]

Other legislation was drawn by Gratian from a papal letter ascribed by him to Pope Clement (c. 88-c. 97. According to ths letter, all priests and clerics who did not obey their Bishop were to be considered as infamous and expelled from the Church.[61] Although this letter was spurious,[62] it had earlier been incorporated in the legislation of the Council of Tribur (895) in canon 8 and duly represented the legislative mind of the Church in the twelfth century.[63]

In another letter supposedly taken from a letter of the same Pope Clement, Gratian stated that all priests, deacons, and all other clerics were forbidden to exercise their orders without the permission of the Bishop.[64] This legislation clearly indicated that the Bishop was the highest authority in the diocese and that all clerics depended upon him for permission to exercise their orders.

(58) "Si quis sacerdotum vel reliquorum clericorum suo episcopo inobediens fuerit, aut ei insidias paraverit, aut contumeliam, aut calumniam, vel convicia intulerit, et convinci potuerit, mox depositus curiae tradatur, et recipiat quod inique gessit."—C. 18, C. XI, q. 1.

(59) *Glossa Ordinaria,* ad c. 18, C. XI, q. 1, s.v. *Si quis sacerdotum.*

(60) *Summa Decretorum,* p. 310.

(61) "Si autem vobis episcopis non obedierint omnes presbyteri, et reliqui clerici . . . non solum infames, sed etiam extorres a regno Dei et a consortio fidelium, et a liminibus sanctae Dei ecclesiae alieni erunt."—c. 11, C. XI, q. 3.

(62) Jaffé, I, 12; Hinschius, *Decretales Pseudo-Isidorianae et Capitula Angilrammi,* p. 52.

(63) Mansi, XVIII, 137.

(64) "Cunctis fidelibus et summopere omnibus presbyteris, et diaconibus, et reliquis clericis attendendum est, ut nihil adsque episcopi licentia proprii agant; non utique missas sine eius iussu quisquam presbyterorum in sua parochia agat, non baptizet, nec quicquam absque eius permissu faciat."—c. 41, C. XVI, q. 1.

Priests were not to celebrate Mass publicly nor to confer baptism without the permission of the Bishop.[65] The permission here referred to was a general permission granted by the Bishop, and not individual permission that needed to be requested in each and every instance.[66]

Although this letter was spurious,[67] its content was apparently incorporated in the Council of Tribur (895) in canon 32,[68] and it too reflected the mind of the Church at that period in history.

In Causa XVIII, Gratian, in order to prove the subjection of clerics to the local Bishop, quoted canon 8 of the Council of Chalcedon (451). This canon stated in part that clerics, when placed over almshouses, monasteries, or shrines of the martyrs were subject to the jurisdiction of the Bishop, and were on no account to presume to withdraw themselves from his jurisdiction.[69]

In legislation taken from canon 8 of the Council of Agde (506), Gratian pointed out that a cleric who abandoned his ecclesiastical office in order to forestall correction from his Bishop and appealed to a secular judge was to be excluded from participation in the services of the Church. The same penalty was levelled against the civil judge if he attempted to defend such a cleric.[70]

SUMMARY

In the passages referred to in Gratian, no new particular legislation concerning the obligation of clerics to obey their Ordinaries is offered. The collection of Gratian were merely a private, not an authentic, collection. The

(65) *Glossa Ordinaria,* ad h.c., s.v. *Missa.*

(66) *Glossa Ordinaria,* ad h.c., s.v. *licentia.*

(67) Jaffé, XI; Hinschius, *Decretales Pseudo-Isidorianae et Capitula Angilrammi,* p. 57.

(68) Mansi, XVIII, 135.

(69) C. 10, C. XVIII, q. 2; cf. *supra,* p. 6.

(70) C. 1, C. XXI, q. 5; cf. *supra,* p. 11.

Decretum never possessed legal authority. However, the prominence which the *Decretum* enjoyed for so long, indicated the mind of the Church at that period. Without being an official codification and notwithstanding its merely private authority, it became the generally accepted digest of ecclesiastical laws, was copied in innumerable manuscripts, consulted in the courts, explained and annotated in the schools.[71]

Article 5. Promises of Pastors and other Beneficed Persons

In the course of the thirteenth and fourteenth centuries a special promise of obedience was prescribed for those who received special positions in the Church. Besides the promises which were exacted of all priests and of all clerics in Major Orders, others also were called for on the part of clerics belonging to definite categories. Thus in the Council of Chateau Gonthier (1231), midway between Laval and Angers in France, a special formulary was prescribed for all clerics who were entrusted with a parish. This formulary demanded that the cleric in question again promise obedience to the Bishop and his officials. This legislation further provided that, if this formula was omitted, the whole procedure was invalid and that the position to which the cleric had been appointed would be considered still vacant.[72]

Similar legislation may be found in the Council of

(71) Stephan Kuttner, "The Father of the Science of Canon Law," *The Jurist* (Washington, D. C. The Catholic University of America School of Canon Law, 1941——), I (1941), 15-19.

(72) Concilium apud Castrum Gonterii (1231), can. 3: "De modo instituendi rectores ecclesiarum et de juramento ipsorum. Statuimus . . . qui antequam tradat instituendae personae curam animarum . . . qua tradita, iterum jurabit quod dioecesano, et aliis magistris suis obediens erit, et ad mandatum suum se faciet ordinari et jura ecclesiae defendet, et alienata revocabit bona fide. Et si ista forma fuit omissa, institutio fiat irrita, et ecclesia pro vacante habeatur."—Hardouin, VII, 192.

Rouen, held in the year 1335. Canon nine of this Council stated that within forty days after taking possession of a benefice the beneficed person had to report to the Bishop or his vicar and make his promise of obedience, fidelity, residence, and other promises as custom prescribed.[73]

In the same year in the Council of Prague a promise of obedience and reverence was likewise required of all beneficed persons. This legislation enumerated the following who were bound to make this profession, namely, any ecclesiastical person, whether regular or secular, who had been constituted or confirmed in any dignity, rank of precedence, office or ecclesiastical position, had personally to make a profession of obedience and reverence to his Superior to observe the provincial and synodical statutes.[74]

Article 6. Decretals of Gregory IX and the Decretalists

Through the assembled decretals of Pope Gregory IX (1227-1241) there appeared one of the earliest collections which enjoyed the force of universal law for the Church.

The first parcel of legislation concerning the canonical obedience of clerics to their Ordinary, as contained in the Decretals of Gregory IX, consisted of a response of Pope Clement III to the Bishop of Ely in England, in which the Pope pointed out that clerics are subject to

(73) "Porro . . . idem institutus, infra quadraginta dies a tempore corporaliter adeptae possessionis, coram diocesano seu eius vicario comparare debet personaliter, fidem facturus debitam de titulo, si quem habet in beneficio sic adepto, ac praestiturus dioecesano de et super obedientia, fidelitate, et residentia, et aliis consuetis debitum et solitum juramentum . . ."—Hardouin, VII, 1607.

(74) "Statuimus etiam quod persona Ecclesiastica quaecumque, regularis aut saecularis, in dignitate, personatu, officio, seu ecclesiastico beneficio quocunque constituatur vel in eodem confirmatur, nisi ante omnia, de obedientia et reverentia suis Superioribus impendenda, de Statutis Provincialibus et Synodalibus, in quantum eam tangunt observandis, corpore praestiterit juramentum."—Hardouin, IV, 389.

their Bishop even before his consecration. Once the Bishop-elect had received the confirmation of his appointment as Bishop, he enjoyed the power to perform all those acts which were just and useful for the diocese, with the exception of acts of the greatest moment, and acts which require the exercise of Orders.

The case in question concerned certain clerics who were laboring under a sentence of suspension or interdict inflicted upon them by the former Bishop. These clerics, making light of the penalty, had left their churches. Some of them even went so far as to lay aside the clerical garb and to take up lay pursuits which involved them in rather questionable commercial transactions. In an effort to resist ecclesiastical correction they offered the excuse that the new Bishop-elect, since he was not yet consecrated, did not possess the power to administer the correction, unless the Apostolic See had furnished him with this power in the form of a special indult.

The response of the Pope stated that if these clerics, after having received a warning, refused to be reconciled with the Church and to be reinstated in the ranks of the clergy, the Bishop-elect certainly possessed the power to level an excommunication against them. The Pope proceeded to inform him that for this procedure he did not need a special mandate, but enjoyed the power to do whatever was right and useful for the government of the Church in his diocese, the performance of the functions that derived from Orders being reserved however until after his consecration.[75]

The Glossator pointed out that while these lay pursuits were licit before entrance into the clerical state, they were not lawful afterwards. He confirmed this by citing chapter 10 of Distinction 88, and chapter 10 of Distinction 31, which made assertions to the same effect.[76]

(75) C. 15, X, *de electione et electi potestate,* I, 6; Jaffé, n. 16572.

(76) *Glossa Ordinaria* ad h.c., s.v. *Mercimonia.*

The Glossator likewise insisted that by the very laying aside of the clerical garb these clerics had automatically lost their clerical privilege, and did not deserve to be defended by the Church.[77]

Baldus de Ubaldis (ca. 1319-1400) made the same observation.[78]

In reference to the powers of the Bishop-elect, the Glossator pointed out that those actions which pertained to jurisdiction, such as that of judging, of excommunicating, of confirming elections, of investing with an office, or of conferring benefices, etc. belonged to the Bishop-elect once his appointment had received confirmation.[79]

Boich (1310-1350) followed the same line of reasoning. He pointed out that the Bishop-elect could suspend, interdict or excommunicate insubordinate clerics if they refused to live according to the rules of the clerical state, since such actions pertained to the realm of jurisdiction, and not to that of Episcopal Orders. The same author pointed out that clerics in Major Orders could be subjected to excommunication solemnly in the presence of other Bishops and of the Chapter. If, however, the clerics in question were in Minor Orders, a solemn excommunication was not required.[80]

The next legislation in the Decretals of Gregory IX was rather succinct. It stated that whoever disobeyed a mandate of the Bishop should be thrown out of the Church.[81] This enactment was taken from a letter of Pope Gregory I (590-604) to Augustine, Bishop of Canterbury.[82] Commenting on this passage, the Glossator

(77) *Glossa Ordinaria* ad h.c., s.v. *Postposito.*

(78) Baldus de Ubaldis, Super Decretalibus (Lugduni, 1547), ad c. 15, X, *de electione et electi potestate,* I, 6.

(79) *Glossa Ordinaria* ad h.c., s.v. *De talibus.*

(80) *Commentaria in Quinque Decretalium Libros* (Venetiis, 1575), ad c. 15, X, *de electione et electi potestate,* I, 6.

(81) C. 2, X, *de maioritate et obedientia,* I, 33.

(82) Jaffé, n. 1829.

stated that a Bishop could make such decrees if they were just.[83]

Hostiensis (+1271) stated the principle that, if one who enjoyed jurisdiction (Bishop) made a just decree, his subjects were bound to follow such a decree. If one disobeyed the injunctions of this decree, he should be expelled from the Church. Hostiensis, however, observed that the postulated disobedience to the decree needed to turn about a serious matter, since the penalty of excommunication was not to be applied unless there was question of a mortal sin.[84] The same author indicated the reason why such a penalty could be applied. The Bishops as the successors of the Apostles commanded the respect and obedience of all their subjects in the Church.[85]

Pope Innocent III (1198-1216), in a letter to the Bishop of Florence, answered a complaint that certain subdeacons maintaned that they were exempt from episcopal jurisdiction because they had been ordained by the Roman Pontiff. The Pope replied that, while the subdeacons did enjoy a privilege of honor by being ordained by the Roman Pontiff, they were by no means absolved from tendering canonical obedience to the Bishop.[86]

In commenting on this passage Hostiensis stated that, notwithstanding their privilege of being ordained by the Roman Pontiff, these clerics were obliged to submit to their bishop for the proper preservation of dignity and honor. Since Bishops were higher in dignity and honor than subdeacons, including the ones ordained by the

(83) *Glossa Ordinaria,* ad c. 2, X, *de maioritate et obedientia,* I, 33. s.v. *Decretum.*

(84) *In Quinque Libros Decretalium Commentaria* (5 vols. in 3, Venetiis, 1581), ad c. 2, X, *de maioritate et obedientia,* I, 33.

(85) *Op. cit.,* ad h.c., s.v. *Principi.*

(86) C. 7, X, *de maioritate et obedientia,* I, 33; Potthast, *Regesta Pontificum Romanorum inde ab anno post Christum natum* MCXCVIII *ad annum* MCCCIV (2 vols., Berolini, 1874-1875), n. 2728 (hereafter referred to as Potthast).

Pope, the latter needed to obey their Bishop.[87]

In another letter of Pope Innocent III, sent on Dec. 31, 1199, to the Bishop of Rossano in southern Italy, a decision was given whereby the Bishop could compel abbots and priests to attend the diocesan synod. In his letter to the Pope, the Bishop complained that certain abbots and priests subject to him by diocesan law refused to be present at the synod, even though the Bishop had called them to it. The reason given by these abbots and priests was that they were not accustomed to attending the synod in the past. The Pope replied that unless the statutes enacted in the synod were contrary to the canonical institutes, the Bishop could compel them by ecclesiastical censures to attend the synod to show the proper obedience and respect to the Bishop.[88]

Commenting on this passage, Hostiensis taught that abbots and priests if entrusted with positions having the care of souls were obliged to attend the synod and to observe the statutes enacted therein; but if not entrusted with the care of souls, they were not obliged to attend.[89]

Panormitanus (1386-1453), in his commentary on this legislation, stated that if the subject matter in the synod dealt with the care of souls or the state of the churches, then those who did not have the care of souls were rightfully excused. However, if the subject matter of the synod dealt with the reformation of morals or with any other subject pertaining to the clergy at large, then all the clerics of the city and the diocese were under obligation to attend, in such a way, however, that the spiritual interests and necessities of the Church would not be impaired.[90]

(87) *In Quinque Libros Decretalium Commentaria,* ad c. 7, X, *de maioritate et obedientia,* I, 33.

(88) C. 9, X, *de maioritate et obedientia,* I, 33.

(89) *In Quinque Libros Decretalium Commentaria,* ad c. 9, X, *de maioritate et obedientia,* I, 33.

(90) *Commentaria in Quinque Libros Decretalium* (5 vols. in 7, Venetiis, 1588), ad c. 9, X, *de maioritate et obedientia,* I, 33.

In another letter of Pope Innocent III, dated July 21, 1199, the Pope wrote to two priors whose monasteries were located in the archdiocese of Braga, in northern Portugal, that he was disappointed in the report that they claimed to be exempt from showing obedience to the Archbishop of Braga. The Pope in very forceful language commanded them to desist from their disobedience, and ordered them, in virtue of his apostolic office, to obey the Archbishop, just as all other clerics were obliged, notwithstanding the accompanying factor of temporal prescription.[91]

Boich in reference to this passage declared that disobedience to one's superior cannot become a warranted usage through the agency of temporal prescription, since it always stands as unreasonable.[92]

Panormitanus stated that a subject at no time became relieved of the burden of obedience to his superior by way of the agency of legal prescription. The reason was this: the Bishop is the head of all in the diocese, and all subordinate prelates continue as members of the body, and hence cannot function without directions from the head.[93]

The next piece of legislation is found in a letter addressed by Pope Honorius III (1216-1227) to all the abbots, prelates, convents, and clerics of the diocese of Constantinople.

John Colosanna, a cardinal priest and legate of the title of St. Praxedes, conferred some monasteries and churches on certain abbots and clerics. They in turn entertained the idea that they did not have to obey the

(91) "Ideoque . . . per apostolica scripta mandamus et in virtute obedientiae districte praecipimus . . . obedientiam et reverentiam debitam, . . . praescriptione temporis non obstante."—c. 12, X, *de praescriptione,* II, 26.

(92) *Commentaria in Quinque Decretalium Libros,* ad c. 12, X, *de praescriptionibus,* II, 26, ad n. 1.

(93) *Commentaria in Quinque Libros Decretalium,* ad c. 12, X, *de praescriptionibus,* II, 26, nn. 1 and 3.

Patriarch. The Pope in a letter of April 7, 1225, corrected this false notion. He stated that even if the spiritual and temporal administration of monasteries and churches had been given over to other churches and clerics apart from the Patriarch and even if this conferral had been made by a Cardinal legate of the Apostolic See and had been confirmed by the Pope, the abbots of these monasteries and churches were not thereby exempt from the obligation of obedience to the Patriarch.(94) Panormitanus commented that a delegate cannot subject one church to another to the prejudice of the Ordinary, and that the Pope, in confirming a delegate's conferral of a benefice, does not wish to infringe upon the rights of the Ordinary. If the Pope wished to take someone under his protection and to confer honors upon him, this does not free the latter from subjection to the jurisdiction of the Ordinary.(95)

Boich stated the principle that, in conferring or confirming a privilege of exemption, the one confirming the privilege does not have the intention of causing prejudice, nor of introducing something new, but rather of conserving the old.(96)

Pope Alexander III (1159-1181) in a letter to the Bishop of London, (others say Tours or Canterbury),(97) declared that if a cleric, while laboring under an interdict or an excommunication inflicted by the Pope or by another Bishop, celebrated the divine offices, he was to be perpetually deposed, unless he repented immediately after being warned.(98) This warning was to be understood

(94) C. 9, X, *de confirmatione utili et inutili,* II, 30; Potthast, n. 7777.

(95) *Commentaria in Quinque Libros Decretalium,* ad c. 9, X, *de confirmatione utilii et inutili,* II, 30.

(96) *Commentaria in Quinque Decretalium Libros,* ad c. 9, X, *de confirmatione utili et inutili,* II, 30, n. 4.

(97) Jaffé, n. 13803.

(98) C. 3, X, *de clerico excommunicato, deposito, vel interdicto ministrante,* V, 27.

dispensative, i.e., if such a cleric repented after he had been duly warned by the Bishop, there was no need for deposing him.[99] Panormitanus stated that if a suspended, interdicted, or excommunicated cleric carried on with his divine offices after having been admonished, he was to be deposed without restraint. However, if the cleric showed signs of repentance and indicated that he wished to correct himself, a warning was not needed, since he had already fulfilled the conditions for absolution.[100]

In a letter of May 21, 1203, Innocent III informed Amedeus, Archbishop of Besançon, that he could deprive clerics of their benefices and, if need be, depose them entirely if they continued to perform their divine offices after having been excommunicated.[101] Panormitanus supplied the reason for this when he stated that any excommunicated priest who presumed to celebrate the divine offices was to be deprived of his benefice, because such an attitude always denoted contumacy; an admonition no longer was necessary. Not only were priests considered as falling under this censure, but also all clerics, even those who were simply in Minor Orders.[102] In commenting on this decretal, Hostiensis stated that such a deprivation was entirely within the rights of the Bishop, since the clerics had not acted reasonably and hence had no right to the restoration of the benefice.[103]

Pope Honorius III (1216-1227) wrote a letter to the Archdeacon of St. Albert, the Abbot of Hainant and the

(99) *Glossa Ordinaria,* ad c. 3, X, *de clerico excommunicato, deposito, vel interdicto ministrante,* V, 27, s.v. *Moniti.*

(100) *Commentaria in Quinque Libros Decretalium,* in c. 3, X, *de clerico excommunicato, deposito, vel interdicto ministrante,* V. 27.

(101) C. 6, X, *de clerico excommunicato, deposito, vel interdicto ministrante,* V. 27; Potthast, n. 1906.

(102) *Commentaria in Quinque Libros Decretalium,* ad c. 6, X, *de clerico excommunicato, deposito, vel interdicto ministrante,* V, 27.

(103) *In Quinque Libros Decretalium Commentaria,* ad c. 6, X, *de clerico excommunicato, deposito, vel interdicto ministrante,* V, 27.

Provost of Cambrai, in which he commanded that the Archdeacon of Amiens be perpetually removed from the church of Amiens, because, contrary to his promise, he had repeatedly refused to recognize the Bishop as his superior and refused to show him proper reverence and obedience. In the absence of the Archdeacon, the Bishop had conferred this benefice upon another whom he deemed worthy of it. The Archdeacon, along with his brother and other accomplices, took the case to a secular court, alleging that he had been unjustly injured. The Pope in very strong language directed that this insubordinate Archdeacon of Amiens be perpetually cut off from the church of Amiens and deprived of all his benefices as a corrupt member, lest he corrupt others.[(104)] The Glossator informs us that the promise made by the Archdeacon was that of fidelity and obedience to his Bishop.[(105)] The Glossator further points out that the Archdeacon automatically denied that the Bishop was his superior by taking the case before a secular judge, and that this constituted a public denial of the Bishop as his superior; thus the Archdeacon needed to be punished.[(106)] In reference to this legislation Panormitanus stated that the Bishop of a diocese can and must be recognized as the master *(dominus)* over his subjects, and that if his subjects refuse to recognize him as such they must be punished severely. This followed from the very fact that clerics had given their promise of obedience and especially admitted in principle that the Bishop is their spiritual master. This they did implicitly in accepting an appointment to a dignity or an assignment to a church.[(107)]

(104) C. X, *de excessibus praelatorum et subditorum,* V, 21.

(105) *Glossa Ordinaria* ad c. 15, X, *de excessibus praelatorum et subditorum,* V, 31, s.v. *Homagii.*

(106) *Glossa Ordinaria* ad c. 15, X, *de excessibus praelatorum et subditorum,* V, 31, s.v. *Negasse.*

(107) *Commentaria in Quinque Libros Decretalium,* ad c. 15, X, *de excessibus praelatorum et subditorum,* V, 31, n. 1.

SUMMARY

Since the promulgation of the Decretals of Gregory IX on the fifth of September, 1234, with the Bull *Rex Pacificus,* invested the collection with universal legal binding force, it might be well here to summarize the legislation contained therein, in order to obtain an idea of the mind of the Church at that period in regard to the relationship between clerics and the Bishop.

1. Clerics were subject to their Bishop, even before the latter's consecration. The only requirements for a Bishop's authority over the clerics of his diocese were that he be appointed and that his appointment be confirmed by the Holy See.

2. Clerics enjoying the privilege of having been ordained by the Roman Pontiff were not exempt from the duty of obedience to the Bishop.

3. Bishops could compel abbots and priests having the care of souls to attend the synod.

4. Clerics laboring under canonical penalties could be deposed if, after being duly warned, they persisted in the performance of ecclesiastical functions or the conducting of divine services.

CHAPTER II

TRIDENTINE AND POST-TRIDENTINE LEGISLATION

Article 1. Legislation of the Council of Trent (1545-1563)

The Church in the first half of the sixteenth century was in a turbulent state of affairs; whole nations under the leadership of Luther, Calvin, Zwingli, Henry VIII, and other so-called reformers had broken off from the one true Church, and, what was worse, internal strife and confusion were threatening the interior order and tranquillity of the Church. Hence, Pope Paul III, (1534-1549), realizing the need of restoring ecclesiastical discipline and restoring the authority of the Church, convoked the Council of Trent on December 13, 1545.

The first legislation enacted in regard to the relationship between the Bishops and the clergy stated that Bishops could conduct a visitation, punish and correct secular priests, notwithstanding whatever personal privileges they might be favored with, and also regulars, even those who enjoyed the privilege of exemption, if they were living outside their monasteries.[1]

In the fourteenth session, the above mentioned legislation was repeated more or less verbatim, with the additional provision that Bishops could, even outside the time of visitation, correct and punish all secular priests, in whatever manner exempt, who would otherwise be subject to the jurisdiction of the Bishop. Chapter IV of this session explicitly stated that secular priests could be punished for their excesses, crimes and delinquencies as often as and whenever there should be need; no exemptions, declarations, customs, sentences, oaths, agreements,

(1) Sess. V, *de ref.*, c. 3; Schroeder, *Canons and Decrees of the Council of Trent* (St. Louis: Herder, 1941), p. 49 (hereafter referred to as Schroeder).

which bound only their authors were to be of any avail to said clerics and their relations, chaplains, domestics, agents, or to any others whatsoever in view and in consideration of said exempt clerics.[2]

It will be noted that in this chapter on reform no reference was made to exempt regulars. This question was again taken up in the twenty-fifth session, where provision was made for a regular not subject to the Bishop and living within the enclosure of a monastery, if outside of that enclosure he had committed so notorious an offence as to be a scandal to the people. At the instance of the Bishop he was to be severely punished by his superior within the time specified by the Bishop, and the superior was to report to the Bishop concerning the punishment. Otherwise he was to be deprived of his office by his superior, and the delinquent regular was to be punished by the Bishop.[3]

Implicitly contained in the legislation of the Council of Trent was the principle that the Bishop is the head of the diocese, and that consequently all the members of the clergy, especially the secular priests, owe him respect and obedience.

Article 2. Jurisprudence of the seventeenth and eighteenth centuries

The commentators of the seventeenth and eighteenth centuries in their treatment of the Decretals of Gregory IX do not shed much new light on the matter of canonical obedience which clerics owe their Ordinary.

Pirhing (1606-1679), commenting on the title *De maioritate et obedientia,* stated that canonical obedience consists mainly in 1) accepting and executing the mandates of the Ordinary, especially those which deal with

(2) Conc. Trident., sess. XIV, *de ref.*, c. 4; Schroeder, p. 108.

(3) Conc. Trident., sess. XXV, *de regularibus,* c. 14; Schroeder, p. 226.

the divine worship or the common good, and 2) submitting oneself to the jurisdiction of one's superior in the judgment and decision of cases.[4]

Fagnanus (1598-1678), and Leurenius (1646-1723), differed slightly in their analysis from that of Pirhing and stated that canonical obedience consists of three factors: 1) showing reverence to one's superior, 2) receiving and carrying out the superior's mandates, and 3) submitting to the superior's judgment.[5]

Reiffenstuel (1642-1703), adhered to the same analysis as Fagnanus and Leurenius.[6]

A considerable variety of opinions existed among the authors of this period concerning the various persons who came under the jurisdiction of the Bishop.

Thus Amort (1692-1775), made the general statement that Bishops have jurisdiction over all secular clerics not only in matters which pertain to divine services and to the administration of the sacraments but also in all things which pertain to the proper conduct of the clergy.[7] He continued with the pointed observation that, since the monastic life neither adds to nor subtracts from the precise nature of the clerical state, it follows that all religious who are likewise clerics, even those who possess the privilege of exemption, are subject to the jurisdiction of

(4) Pirhing, *Jus Canonicum, Nova Methodo Explicatum, Omnibus Capitulis Titulorum* (5 vols. in 3,, Dilingae, 1722), Lib. I, tit, XXXIII, c. II, n. 7 (hereafter referred to as Pirhing).

(5) Fagnanus, *Commentaria in Quinque Libros Decretalium* (5 vols., Romae, 1661), Lib. I, *de maioritate et obedientia, C. IX;* Leurenius, Jus *Canonicum Universum* (5 vols. in 4, Venetiis, 1729), Lib. I, tit. XXXIII, q. dccexiii, n. 2.

(6) Reiffenstuel, *Jus Canonicum Universum* (5 vols. in 7, Parisiis, 1864-1870), Lib. I, tit. XXXIII, n. 15 (hereafter referred to as Reiffenstuel).

(7) Amort, *Elementa Iuris Canonici Veteris et Moderni* (3 vols. Ferrariae, 1763), III, Diss. VI *de iurisdictione episcoporum,* n. IX (hereafter referred to as Amort).

the Bishop relative both to ecclesiastical discipline and to the proper conduct of the members of the clerical state.[8]

The authors of this period were almost in complete agreement in asserting that all clerics, when entrusted with the care of souls, were, according to the custom prevailing in the Church, obliged, on the occasion of their installation, to make a promise of obedience to their Bishop.[9] Clerics who were not entrusted with the care of souls or with positions of administration satisfied their obligation if they made their promise of obedience verbally or manually.[10] If in these circumstances the Bishop demanded the promise of obedience in the form of writing or in the form of an oath, he exceeded the limits of his office, thereby running the risk of injuring the cleric. Accordingly, the cleric was not obliged to obey this demand of the Bishop.[11] However, if a cleric had been disobedient, rebellious, contumacious, or even suspect of disobedience, he could be compelled to make an oath of obedience to the Bishop.[12]

The Bishop's jurisdiction over all the parishes within his diocese was taken for granted by the canonists of this period. This is apparent from the fact that they stressed the Bishop's jurisdiction over parishes held by religious and passed over the consideration of such as were en-

(8) Amort, *ibid.*, n. X.

(9) Schmalzgrueber, *Jus Ecclesiasticum Universum* (5 vols. in 12, Romae, 1843-1845), Lib. I, tit. XXXIII, n. 15 (hereafter referred to as Schmalzgrueber); Pirhing, Lib. I, tit. XXXIII, n. XX; Pichler, *Candidatus Iurisprudentiae Sacrae* (4. ed., 5 vols., Ingolstadii, 1724-1728), Lib. I, tit. XXXIII, n. 7 (hereafter referred to as Pichler).

(10) According to Fagnanus, "manually" indicated that the promise was not given in writing.—Lib. I, *de maioritate et obedientia,* n. 7.

(11) Schmalzgrueber, *ibid.,* n. 2; Pichler, *loc. cit.;* Leurenius, Lib. I, tit. XXXIII, q. dccccxvi.

(12) Schmalzgrueber, *loc. cit.*

trusted to the secular clergy. Thus, if a religious had charge of a parish which was subject to the Bishop, he had to obey the Bishop in all matters pertaining to the proper administration and the care of souls.[13] Pichler pointed out that in those matters which pertain to the rule of the religious life the religious was not subject to the Bishop, but to his own religious superior. But, in the event that the religious superior was negligent, then the Bishop could demand obedience.[14]

In regard to the diocesan synod, priests who were under the jurisdiction of the diocesan Bishop had to attend the diocesan synod and to obey the statutes enacted therein. Furthermore, if they refused to attend the diocesan synod after having been summoned by the Bishop, the latter could compel them by ecclesiastical censure to attend.[15] Even exempt abbots and regulars had to attend the diocesan synod if they had the care of souls and were summoned by the Bishop.[16]

The most complete treatment of the relationship between the Bishop and his clergy is that given by Reiffenstuel. Commenting on the title *De maioritate et obedientia* of the Decretals of Gregory IX, he laid down the following principles:

1) If there were a doubt whether the command of a superior was contrary to the law of God or not, the superior had to be obeyed. The principle he supported with the

(13) Pichler, Lib. I, tit. XXXIII, n. 8; Leurenius, Lib. I, tit. XXXIII, q. dccccxv.

(14) Pichler, Lib. I, tit. XXXIII, n. 8.

(15) Pirhing, Lib. I, tit. XXXIII, C. VII, n. 1; Barbosa, *Collectanea Doctorum tam Veterum quam Recentiorum in Ius Pontificium Universum* (6 vols., Lugduni, 1656), Lib. I. tit. XXXIII, C. II, n. 2 (hereafter referred to as Barbosa); Fagnanus, Lib. I, *de maioritate et obedientia,* n. 2; Leurenius, Lib. I, tit. XXXIII, q. dccccxv, n. 3.

(16) Pirhing, *loc. cit.; Fagnanus,* Lib. I, *de maioritate et obedientia,* C. IX; Pichler, Lib. I, tit. XXXIII, n. 2; Leurenius, Lib. I. tit. XXXIII, q. dccccxv, n. 3.

axiom, *"In dubio, melior est conditio possidentis."* In this case, the superior commanding held a more juridical right than the doubting subject. Although the superior may have acted wrongly by issuing a particular command, the subject acted rightly in obeying his superior's command.(17)

2) If a superior ordered something directly contrary to God's law, a subject certainly was not under any obligation of obeying. To confirm this principle, he quoted the words of Saint Peter, "We ought to obey God rather than man." (Acts 5, 29) (18)

3) If one was subject to two superiors, he had to obey the one who held a greater measure of power over him.(19) To illustrate this principle, he pointed out that a cleric was to obey his Bishop rather than the Archbishop, because the latter had no direct jurisdiction over the cleric inasmuch as he could not command the subject of a suffragan Bishop, without first consulting the latter.(20)

Finally, concerning the penalties levelled against disobedient clerics, the legislation at this period was quite definite.

1) Those clerics who contumaciously disobeyed the decrees and statutes of the Bishop were subject to the penalty of excommunication. However, this penalty was to be inflicted only in cases of grave fault on the part of the cleric. But it could be inflicted even in matter of lesser moment, if the element of contumacy was present.

(17) Reiffenstuel, *ibid.*, n. 18.

(18) Reiffenstuel, *ibid.*, n. 19.

(19) Reiffenstuel, *ibid.*, n. 22.

(20) Reiffenstuel, *ibid.*, n. 23; cf. also Leurenius, Lib. I, tit. XXXIII, q. dccccxviii.

2) Those clerics who did not observe the canonical constitutions incurred infamy, but if the sin itself was forgiven, then the infamy also was taken away upon the performance of the prescribed penance.[21]

Article 3. Legislation of Particular and Plenary Councils

Following the example of the Council of Trent, many provincial councils and synods throughout the world began to incorporate statutes and decrees concerning the canonical obedience which clerics owed their Ordinaries. Thus in the Provincial Council of Avignon, held in the year 1725, the directors of Seminaries were instructed to strive to inculcate not only the other qualities required of men preparing for the priesthood, but especially the proper reverence and obedience which they owed their Bishop, because these co-ordinated and strengthened the ecclesiastical order in the same way as the proper function of the nerves co-ordinated the operations of the body.[22]

The Provincial Council of Gran, Hungary (1858), adopted the same figure of speech in its statutes on the canonical obedience and reverence which clerics owe their Ordinary.[23]

The Synod of Mount Lebanon, Syria (1736), stated explicitly that of the directions or prohibitions contained in its constitutions and decrees only those constituted grave matter whose very nature made it evident, or where observance was commanded under holy obedience, or in connection with which the penalty of suspension or ex-

(21) Schmalzgrueber, Lib. I, tit. XXXIII, n. 18; Leurenius, *ibid.*, q. dccccxx; Pirhing, Lib. I, tit. XXXIII, C. VII, n. 27.

(22) Concilium Provinciale Avenionensis (1725), tit. XXXIII, C. I, *Acta et Decreta Sacrorum Conciliorum Recentiorum, Collectio Lacensis* (7 vols., Friburgi Brisgoviae, 1870-1892), I, 53 (hereafter referred to as *Coll. Lac.*).

(23) Tit. IX, n. 2—*Coll. Lac.*, V, 82.

communication was threatened for the refusal to carry them out, or, finally, in relation to which any contempt or obstinacy would become a source of scandal.[24]

In the same Provincial Council, missionaries were directed to obey the Prefect of the missions. In all matters which pertained to the proper administration of the missions, the missionaries were by means of a letter, and if possible, even by personal interview to seek the counsel of, and to work in conjunction and concord with their ecclesiastical superior for the propagation of the faith in the missions. It was no more than proper that the missionaries obey the Patriarch and the local Ordinaries and abide by their decisions. Without first obtaining the permission of their Ordinaries, the missionaries were not to presume to preach, to administer the sacraments, or to perform other ecclesiastical functions.[25]

In the I Provincial Council of Baltimore (1829), it was stated that priests who exercised their ministry in the United States of America were removable from their churches or missions at the discretion of the Bishop. The Council had based its interpretation on the solemn promise of obedience made by the priests when they were ordained. Therefore, in the first decree it was stated that, in virtue of the promise made at ordination, priests were obliged to obey the Bishop in the assignment to any mission. In this matter the Council was referring to the Epistle *Ex quo* of Pope Benedict XIV, given under date of January 14, 1747. In this Epistle Pope Benedict quite explicitly stated that the solemn promise of obedience and reverence (which the priest makes with his hands enclosed within the Bishop's, on the occasion of his ordination, according to a very ancient practice of the Church) was not an empty and meaningless formula.

(24) Cap. VII, n. 2—*Coll. Lac.*, II, 408.
(25) Appendix, Cap. V,—*Coll. Lac.*, II, 457.

Indeed the priest in virtue of this promise, among other things, was obliged to give his services to the Church for which he was ordained, and he was not to leave this church without the permission of his Bishop.

The legislation of the I Provincial Council of Baltimore, however, had interpreted the words of Pope Benedict in a wider sense than was warranted. The Sacred Congregation called this to the attention of the Fathers of the Council of Baltimore and advised them to change the legislation from ". . . in virtue of the promise of obedience . . . priests are obliged to obey the Bishop in the assignment to any mission," to read, ". . . priests, mindful of the promise made on the occasion of their ordination, are not to leave any mission to which they are assigned by the Bishop."(26)

The II Plenary Council of Baltimore (1866), repeated this legislation from the I Provincial Council of Baltimore with the added provision that the Bishop was to provide for the adequate sustenance of the priests appointed to the missions.(27)

The III Plenary Council of Baltimore (1884), confirmed the legislation of the I Provincial and the II Plenary Councils of Baltimore on this point.(28)

(26) Instructio—*Coll. Lac.*, III, 22; *Concilia Provincialia Baltimori Habita ab anno* 1829 *usque ad annum* 1849 (Ed. altera, Baltimori, John Murphy, 1851), p. 64.

(27) ". . . monemus omnes sacerdotes in hisce dioecesibus degentes, sive fuerint in iis ordinati, sive in easdem co-optati, ut memores promissionis in ordinatione emissae, non detrectent vacare cuilibet missioni ab episcopo designatae, si episcopus judicet sufficiens ad vitae decentem sustentationem subsidium illic haberi posse, idque manus viribus et valetudini sacerdotum ipsorum convenire"—*Concilii Plenarii Baltimorensis II, in Ecclesia Metropolitana Baltimorensi, a die VII ad diem XXI Octobris, A.D. MDCCCLXVI, Habiti et a Sede Apostolica Recogniti, Acta et Decreta* (Baltimorae, John Murphy, 1868), tit, III, C. IV, n. 108.

(28) ". . . quemlibet sacerdotem qui pro quacumque huius provinciae diocesi ordinatus fuerit, teneri vi promissionis in ordinatione factae ad permanendum in eadem dioecesi, et ad se subjiciendum praesuli suo, usquedum canonice dimissus fuerit."—*Acta et Decreta Concilii Plenarii*

Several provincial councils in their statutes explicitly referred to the promise of obedience which priests made to the Bishop on the occasion of their ordination. Thus the Council of Albi, France (1850), in its decrees enacted the following legislation:

"Obedientiae et reverentiae quas sacratissimo ordinationis die professi sunt memores, Statutorum et Mandatorum episcopalium sint observantissimi . . ." (29)

The Provincial Council of Toulouse, France (1850), likewise in relying on the promise of obedience made to the Bishop on the day of ordination directed pastors studiously to fulfill the offices entrusted to them.(30)

The same exhortation was employed by the Provincial Council of Bordeaux, France (1850), which placed filial obedience to the Bishop's mandates on an even basis with the charity which members of the clergy owe their Bishop.(31)

The Provincial Council of Ravenna, Italy (1855), after referring to the promise made at sacred ordination, exhorted all priests, especially the ones entrusted with the care of souls, studiously and constantly to fulfill their offices in obedience and reverence. Furthermore, they were admonished to hold in reverence, not only the person of the Bishop but likewise all his acts, commands, and decrees. In a paternal admonition all clerics and priests were urged to consult with the Bishop in arduous and

Baltimorensis Tertii, A.D. MDCCCLXXXIV (Baltimorae, John Murphy, 1886), tit. II, Cap. VII, n. 60.

(29) Decretum V, n. 7.—*Coll. Lac.,* IV, 412.

(30) Tit. I, Cap. VI, n. xxxviii,—*Coll. Lac.,* IV, 1042.

(31) Tit. IV, Cap. XII, n. 6.—*Coll. Lac.,* IV, 590.

perplexing questions, and to obey his salutary mandates and admonitions in a humble and submissive spirit.[32]

The Provincial Council of Urbino, Italy (1859), incorporated the same legislation in its statutes.[33]

By quoting the words of St. Bernard, "Let the priests not disdain to be subject to their Superior if they wish to follow a more secure course," the Provincial Council of Sens, France (1850), and the II Provincial Council of Quebec, Canada (1854), prefaced their legislation, concerning the conduct of the clergy. Following this exhortation, the priests would avoid whatever the Bishop forbade and execute promptly, humbly and faithfully whatever he commanded.[34]

An interesting piece of legislation is found in the Provincial Council of Kalócsa, Hungary (1863), which noted that even resigned or retired priests were by no means to consider themselves exempt from the sacred obligation of obedience to the Ordinary. Indeed, they too needed faithfully to observe the canons and the diocesan statutes, particularly those which governed the conduct of the clergy.[35]

The Provincial Council of Utrecht (1865), after reminding the clergy of the reverence and obedience which they owed the Bishop, proceeded to describe the relationship which should exist between the clergy and the Bishop. The clergy should look upon their divinely constituted Pastor, both as their spiritual father and brother, whose words should be hearkened to in a spirit of love, and whose admonitions and directions should be reverently received and faithfully carried out.[36]

(32) Cap. V, n. VIII.—*Coll. Lac.*, VI, 200.
(33) Tit. VI, n. cxlii,—*Coll. Lac.* VI, 48.
(34) Tit. IV,—*Coll. Lac.*, IV, 904; Cap. XIV, 10—*Coll. Lac.*, III, 651.
(35) Tit. IV, Cap. XV.—*Coll. Lac.*, V, 686.
(36) Tit. VIII, Cap. IV.—*Coll. Lac.*, V, 907.

Article 4. Papal Legislation and Replies from the Roman Congregations

Section 1. Papal Legislation

Pope Benedict XIV (1740-1758), in a constitution reaffirmed one point concerning episcopal jurisdiction, namely, that the Bishop is the head of the diocese and that all ecclesiastical functions within that diocese are dependent upon his permission. Certain exempt priest-religious who neither enjoyed the status of pastors nor were entrusted with the care of souls, went about assisting at marriages without the permission of the local Bishop or the pastor. Apparently this practice was not uncommon, for this abuse was brought to the attention of the Congregations in Rome on more than one occasion. The question was asked whether it was within the jurisdiction of the religious superior, or of the Bishop, to correct this abuse.

Citing the legislation of the Council of Trent (Sessio XXIV, *de ref.* c. 4) and the constitution of Gregory XV, *Inscrutabili,* of February 5, 1622, Pope Benedict pointed out that matters which pertain to the administration of the diocese pertain to the jurisdiction of the local Ordinary. The whole question of the Bishop's jurisdiction over the religious, even exempt religious, was summed up as follows: Whatever the Bishop can demand from a secular pastor he can and must demand from a religious pastor, and whatever decrees the Bishop does enact, he can likewise enforce with ecclesiastical sanctions.[37]

The principle underlying the exemption of religious from the jurisdiction of the local Ordinary was very pointedly brought out in a constitution of Pope Leo XIII, of May 8, 1881. In this constitution Pope Leo pointed out that the fundamental principle of exemption from the

(37) Benedictus XIV, const. *Firmandis,* 6 nov. 1744 §3, §10—*Fontes,* n. 349.

local Ordinary definitely does not center about the concept that the members of Religious Orders enjoy a better position than the secular clergy in this respect, but rather that, by a fiction of law, their monasteries are to be considered as lying in a territory withdrawn from the diocese and that they are immediately subject to the Roman Pontiff, and as such are exempt from the jurisdiction of the Bishop by a special privilege. (Vatican Council, const. *Pastor Aeternus,* Cap. 3, 1870). However, when in fact these exempt religious lived outside the monastery within the confines of the diocese, the tenor of this privilege was tempered, and the religious became subject to the Bishop's power, both ordinary and delegated, so that the diocesan discipline might be maintained.[38]

Pope Gregory XVI (1831-1846), in an encyclical addressed to all the Patriarchs, Archbishops, and Bishops of the Universal Church, urged all priests to obey their Bishops. During the reign of this Pope the Church was, from the human outlook at least, in a difficult way. Religious tyranny and persecution of the Catholic Church was rampant in Switzerland. The Pontiff apparently foresaw the bitter persecution of the Church in Spain and Portugal which was threatening, and which actually broke out in all its fury within a year's time. Finally, the Carbonari were threatening to overthrow Italy.

The Pope commenced his encyclical on a note of sadness, pointing out the evils of the time, and mentioned among the other evils the neglect of the obedience which is due to the Bishops and the wanton infringement of their rights. Hence, the Holy Father exhorted all priests to be subject to their Bishops, upon whom they should look as their spiritual fathers. Clerics were not to forget that they were forbidden by the sacred canons to undertake any ministry, teaching, or preaching without the direction of the Bishop, for the Bishop had the care of all the

(38) Leo XIII, const. *Romanos Pontifices,* 8 maii 1881, 7—*Fontes,* n. 582.

people within his diocese and himself was subject to the rendering of an account of their souls. (This was a reference to the *Canones Apostolorum*, n. 38).[39]

In an encyclical to the Archbishop Primate, Bishops, clerics, Religious, and Faithful of the Catholic Armenian nation within the Province of Constantinople, Pope Pius IX (1846-1878), exhorted all members of the clergy to be mindful of their duty of canonical obedience. In this encyclical the Pope reminded all the members of the clergy that upon their entrance into the clerical state they had chosen the Lord for their inheritance. Therefore they should be subject to and obey their proper Ordinaries, as the only right and fitting practice, since they are His representatives in the Church. And in order that the Church may be built up and strengthened, the clergy were exhorted to be mindful of their calling and dignity, and to conduct themselves accordingly in their deportment and holiness of life.[40]

Pope Leo XIII (1878-1903), in an encyclical to the Church in Spain, pointed out the position of the Bishop in the economy of the Church. Just as the Supreme Pontiff is the supreme teacher and ruler over the whole Church, so the Bishop is the ruler and head of the Church in his respective diocese. Hence it is the prerogative of the Bishop to govern, command, and correct, and in general to provide for everything which he deems necessary for the promotion of the Church in his diocese.

Although this encyclical was primarily intended for the faithful of Spain, the Holy Father made specific reference to the clergy, in that they should set the example.

> ". . . Ac nominatim vehementer studeant modestiam atque obedientiam tenere qui sunt ex ordine Cleri, quorum dicta factaque utique ad exemplum in omnes partes valent plurimum . . ."

(39) Gregorius XVI, ep. encycl. *Mirori vos*, 15 aug. 1832, §5, §8—*Fontes*, n. 485.

(40) Pius IX, ep. encycl. *Neminem vestrum*, 2 febr. 1854, n. 6—*Fontes*, n. 516.

Finally, clerics were exhorted to follow the directions of the Bishop in the undertaking of any projects which affected the discipline and order of the diocese.[41]

In another encyclical to the Bishops and faithful in France, Pope Leo XIII stressed the authority of the Bishop in the government of the diocese. In this encyclical the Pope summarized the whole question of canonical obedience on the part of priests to their Bishop with the following statement: "The sacerdotal office will not be holy, useful or propitious for the future unless it is exercised under the authority and guidance of the Bishop."[42]

On September 2, 1893, Pope Leo XIII issued an encyclical to the Bishops of Hungary in which he indicated the relationship which should exist between the members of the clerical state and their Bishop. The clergy should adhere to their Bishop, accept his admonitions and counsels, assist him in his various undertakings; and in the acceptance and performance of their sacred offices, and in their labors for the salvation of souls, they should always be prompt and cheerful, and devote themselves to them in the spirit of charity.[43]

Six years later, Pope Leo XIII wrote another encyclical letter to the Archbishops, Bishops, and Clergy in France. In the matter concerning the obedience which clerics owe their Ordinary, it was very similar to the one addressed to the clergy in Hungary. The Holy Father pointed out in this encyclical letter that clerics would avoid inconveniences, embarassment and spiritual disaster if they conformed their actions to the established discipline of the Church. This ecclesiastical discipline demanded a union between the various members of the hierarchy, and respect

(41) Leo XIII, ep. encycl. *Cum Multa,* 8 dec. 1882, nn. 4,5,—*Fontes,* n. 587.

(42) Leo XIII, ep. encycl. *Nobilissima,* 8 febr. 1884, n. 9—*Fontes,* n. 590.

(43) Leo XIII, ep. encycl. *Constanti Hungarorum,* 2 sept. 1893, n. 9—*Fontes,* n. 620.

and obedience on the part of inferiors to their superiors.[44]

Three years later Pope Leo XIII issued another encyclical letter to the Bishops of Italy, in which he made reference to the duty of canonical obedience of the clergy to their Ordinary. In this encyclical letter he pointed out that this spirit of obedience should be inculcated in the seminary. He directed a general admonition to priests, exhorting them to be obedient to their Bishops, who have been appointed by the Holy Spirit to guide the Church.[45]

Pope Pius X (1903-1914), issued to all members of the Catholic clergy an exhortation in which he described the ideal of the priesthood and pointed out, among other duties and obligations connected herewith, the obligation of canonical obedience which clerics owe their Bishops.[46]

Section 2. Replies from the Roman Congregations

The Sacred Congregation for the Propagation of the Faith, in an instruction to the Vicar Apostolic of China, made it quite clear that European missionaries were fully dependent upon the Bishop and hence had the duty to obey him always and everywhere, as they professed before they received their appointment to the mission, or publicly in their reception of Holy Orders. This subjection they had to acknowledge by observing the established obedience to the rules and laws which the Ordinaries had deemed fit to enact for the good of the mission effort.[47]

The following questions were submitted to the Sacred Congregation of the Council by the Bishop of Toulouse:

(44) Leo XIII, litt. encycl. *Depuis le jour,* 8 sept. 1899, nn. 2,3—*Fontes,* n. 642.

(45) Leo XIII, litt. encycl. *Fin dal principio,* 8 dec. 1902, n. 7—*Fontes,* n. 650.

(46) Pius X, exhortatio *Haerent animo,* 4 aug. 1908—*Fontes,* n. 683.

(47) S.C. de Prop. Fide, inst. (ad Vic. Ap. Sin.), 18 oct. 1883—*Fontes,* n. 4903; *Collectanea Sacrae Congregationis de Propoganda Fide* (2 vols., Romae: Typographia Polyglotta S.C.P.F., 1907), n. 1606.

1) May priests, enjoying good health, who are assigned to chapels of ease, but who prefer a more easy and carefree life, renounce these chapels of ease (since strictly speaking they are not benefices), and repair to the Episcopal See city or other larger cities of the diocese, before their resignation has been accepted by the Bishop?

   Such conduct, the Bishop pointed out, resulted in scandal in the eyes of the laity; moreover, the people and many churches were consequently left without any priest. The Bishop pleaded a shortage of priests.

   The Sacred Congregation responded in the negative.

2) May the Bishop by a precept of obedience, and under pain of censures, compel such priests to return, to resume their duties, and to remain until the Bishop can provide successors?

The Sacred Congregation responded in the affirmative, but annexed several conditions. The Bishop could, even with censures, compel priests who enjoy good health and are free from other duties to take care of these churches until the Bishop can provide otherwise.[48]

In a reply of the Sacred Congregation of the Council on August 6, 1910, to the Bishop of St. Jean de Maurienne, a similar response was given. The priests in question alleged the following reasons why they should not be forced to remain in the small churches to which they had been assigned:

1) The promise of obedience to the Ordinary on the day of ordination does not oblige to such an inconvenience. If they knew this beforehand they would not have made this promise.

[48] S.C.C., *Tolosana,* 9 maii 1884, nn. 1,2,3—*Fontes,* n. 4263; cf. S.C.C., *Parmen,* 17 ian. 1886, nn. 2,3,4—*Fontes,* n. 4268; also cf. S.C.C., *Foroiulien,* 31 ian. 1891,—*Fontes,* n. 4283.

2) Such an appointment entailed too difficult a position in such trying times.

3) The tediousness of begging for sustenance proved too trying a hardship.

4) The ungrateful attitude of the people made their life most unhappy.

5) Ill health was the ultimate outcome of this state of things.

The Bishop asked if he could, if need be, with ecclesiastical censures, constrain those priests, when he judged them capable and worthy, to take over these parishes.

The Sacred Congregation answered in the affirmative, provided that the priests were actually in good health, and provided that the Bishop could not make provision for these vacant churches in any other way.[49]

(49) S.C.C., *S. Ioannis Maurianae,* 6 aug. 1910—*AAS,* II (1910), 911.

PART II

CANONICAL COMMENTARY

CHAPTER III

SUBJECTS AND OBJECTS OF CANONICAL REVERENCE AND OBEDIENCE

Article 1. Definitions of Reverence and Obedience in Canon Law

After the Code of Canon Law has treated the notion of the interior life which clerics are expected to lead, it takes up the regulations which govern the exterior life of the cleric. Canon 127 states that all clerics, but especially priests, are bound by a special obligation to show reverence and obedience each to his own Ordinary. The Code speaks of a *special* obligation on the part of clerics to distinguish their particular duty from the general obligation which is incumbent upon all the faithful.[1] It is notewothy that the Code includes all clerics without making any distinction between secular or religious, or between the various ranks of the clergy. Hence every person who has received the clerical tonsure, or any or all of the Minor and Major Orders on up through the ranks of the Priesthood and the Episcopate, owe reverence and obedience to their respective Ordinaries. These various phases of reverence and obedience will be treated more fully in the course of this study.

Reverence

Before proceding with the notion of the attendant obligations, it is proper to define and explain the terms "reverence" and "obedience" in Canon Law. Various definitions and explanations of the term "reverence" are given by the various authors, but in the final analysis they all agree in substance. Thus Beste rather explains than

(1) Ojetti, *Commentarium in Codicem Iuris Canonici* (4 vols., Romae, 1927-1931), II, 91.

defines the term "reverence" as implying those exterior signs of honor by which subordinates acknowledge the dignity and authority of their superiors, e.g., by kissing their hand or ring, by rising in their presence, etc.[2] A similar explanation of this term is given by Wernz (1842-1914),-Vidal (1867-1938), who stated that "reverence" refers to that respect and deference which a subordinate owes his superior. Canonical reverence is manifested particularly by means of a deferential conduct in one's speech to the superior or regarding him, and through the use of a certain conventional etiquette in his presence, such as the act of kissing his ring or his hand, or of rising upon his approach, etc. .[3] A more scientific definition is the one that is given by moral theologians, who define reverence as *"virtus moralis, qua superioribus et personis in dignitate constitutis debitus cultus exhibetur."* [4] In discussing this virtue in general, Noldin indicated that one phase of this virtue has reference to the subject under discussion. After treating this subject of reverence from the civil aspect, he referred to reverence in the religious sphere, as in the case of reverence for the Supreme Pontiff and for the Bishops.[5]

The origin of this duty of respect on the part of clerics arises from the nature of the hierarchical order in the Church. Those who are dedicated to the divine ministry at least by first tonsure are called clerics. They are not all of the same grade, but there is a sacred hierarchy among them, some being subordinated to others. By

(2) Beste, *Introductio in Codicem* (3. ed. Collegeville, Minnesota: St. John's Abbey Press, 1946), p. 182.

(3) Wernz-Vidal, *Ius Canonicum ad Codicis Norman Exactum* (7 vols. in 8, Vol. I, ed. altera, 1952; Vol. II, 3. ed., a P. Aguirre recognita, 1943; Vol. III, 1933; Vol. VII, ed. altera, 1951, Romae: Apud Aedes Universitatis Gregorianae, II, n. 92 (hereafter referred to as *Ius Canonicum*).

(4) Noldin-Schmitt, *Summa Theologiae Moralis* (27. ed., 3 vols., Vol. II, *De Praeceptis*, Oeniponte, 1950), II, p. 259, n. 277 (hereafter referred to as *De Praeceptis*).

(5) Noldin-Schmitt, *De Praeceptis, loc. cit.* n. 2.

divine institution, the sacred hierarchy as regards Orders consists of Bishops, priests, and ministers; as regards jurisdiction, it consists of the supreme pontificate and the subordinate episcopate; other grades have been added to these by ecclesiastical institution.[6] Every member of the Church has the obligation to show proper respect to clerics according to their various grades and offices.[7] Clerics, in turn, in virtue of Canon 127, have a special obligation to show reverence to their own Ordinary. This special obligation arises from the element of their ordination to higher orders and their possesson of higher positions in the Church. First and foremost, reverence is due to the Supreme Pontiff, for as successor to the primacy of St. Peter, the Roman Pontiff has not only the primacy *of honor* but also supreme and *full power of jurisdiction* over the universal Church in matters of faith and morals as well as in matters pertaining to the discipline and government of the Church throughout the whole world. This power is episcopal, ordinary, and immediate, and extends over each and every church, and over each and every pastor, as well as over each and every member of the faithful, and is independent of all human authority.[8] It follows that all clerics owe reverence in the first place to the Supreme Pontiff.

Next in line in the hierarchy of Orders is the episcopate. Again, all the faithful, hence all clerics, owe respect to all Bishops of the Church. Thus all clerics, secular or religious, exempt or non-exempt, have the general obligation of showing reverence to each and every Bishop, regardless of whether or not they are subject to his jurisdiction. On the other hand, Superiors of Religious Orders and Institutes, unless they have been elevated to the episcopate, would not merit the same reverence on the part of all clerics but only that reverence which is

(6) Can. 108.
(7) Can. 119.
(8) Can. 218.

due all priests. These Superiors would merit a special reverence on the part of all their subjects. Whereas all clerics are bound to respect all Bishops, Canon 127 implies a special respect for their own Ordinary. The reason for this is quite obvious, since these clerics, and particularly priests, work in closer co-operation with their Ordinary for the care of souls.

Although this will be treated later on in this work, it might be well to indicate that the Church zealously guards this reverence which is due to all clerics and has provided serious sanctions to be levelled against those who violate it.[9]

Obedience

Obedience in general is defined by one moral theologian as *"virtus moralis, qua voluntati superioris obtemperamus."*[10] Although this is a general definition, it may very well serve the present purpose, for canonical obedience simply limits the field to particular superiors and particular subordinates. As related to Canon Law, various applications and explanations have been offered by the commentators. Thus Beste states that canonical obedience consists in that submission and compliance which clerics are bound to show their superiors.[11] The obedience which a secular cleric or priest owes his Ordinary is called *canonical obedience,* in contradistinction to religious obedience, because it does not extend beyond those things which are prescribed by Canon Law.[12]

(9) Cf. Can. 2344 and Can. 2345.

(10) Noldin-Schmitt, *De Praeceptis,* II, p. 260, n. 278.

(11) *Introductio in Codicem,* p. 182.

(12) Raus, *De Sacrae Obedientiae Virtute et Voto* (Lugduni, 1923), p. 29, n. 1; Augustine, *A Commentary on the New Code of Canon Law* (8 vols., Vol. II, 2. ed., 1919; Vol. III, 3. ed. 1922, St. Louis: Herder & Co.) Vol. II, p. 72 (hereafter referred to as Augustine, *A Commentary*).

Article 2. Dominative Power and Jurisdiction

Dominative power consists in the authority of the superior to direct the members of a religious body to the end for which the Institute was founded, and is therefore confined to the scope of the Institute itself and limited by its Constitutions and Rules.[13]

All Religious Superiors have dominative power over their subjects. Dominative power may arise naturally, as the power of the head of a family, or it may arise through an agreement by which a person subjects himself to the rule of another. This dominative power as exercised in Religious Institutes may therefore be defined as *that authority which a superior has over his subjects in virtue of their enrollment in the community, and by reason of which he governs their actions, within limits defined by the Code of Canon Law and the particular Constitutions of the Institute, to the attainment of the end or purpose of the Institute.*[14] The author here cited has inserted into his definition the remote source of this dominative power, "*in virtue of their enrollment in the community.*" There seems to be a divergence of opinions in this matter. Some authors maintain that this dominative power arises from the private wills of those who form the Religious Institute;[15] some claim this arises from the vow of obedience;[16] some from the quasi-

(13) Augustine, *A Commentary,* Vol. III, p. 104.

(14) Clancy, *The Local Religious Superior,* The Catholic University of America Canon Law Studies, n. 175 (Washington, D. C.: The Catholic University of America Press, 1943), p. 8 (hereafter referred to as Clancy, *The Local Religious Superior*).

(15) E.g., Fanfani, *De Iure Religiosorum ad Norman Iuris Canonici* (2. ed., Taurini-Romae: Marietti, 1925), n. 51.

(16) E.g., Berutti *Institutiones Iuris Canonici* (5 vols., Taurini-Romae: Marietti, 1936-1943), III, *De Religiosis,* n. 23 (hereafter referred to as Berutti, *Institutiones*).

contract of religious profession;[17] and others from the natural law, which confers upon every legitimately established society the authority necessary for its direction and conservation.[18]

Regardless of the opinion to which one may subscribe, one fact stands out, namely, that this dominative power as vested in Religious Superiors is not an essential power of the Church but rather a power proper to an imperfect or subordinate society. Of itself this dominative power does not imply a legislative, judicial or executive power in the fullest sense. It does, however, contain the power to command, to investigate, and to punish. But, since it is not actually ecclesiastical jurisdiction, Religious Superiors of such Institutes may not enact new laws, conduct trials, or impose more severe penalties than such as are specified in the Code of Canon Law or in the Constitutions of their particular Institute.[19]

Jurisdiction

Ecclesiastical jurisdiction is the power to govern the faithful for the supernatural end for which the Church was established by Christ. This power is in the Church by divine institution, since Christ with a divine authority conferred it upon the Church.[20]

(17) E.g., Coronata, *Institutiones Iuris Canonici ad Usum Utriusque Cleri et Scholarum* (4 vols., Taurini, Marietti, 1928-1935) I, n. 527 (hereafter referred to as Coronata, *Institutiones*).

(18) Wernz-Vidal, *Ius Canonicum*, III, n. 93; Cappello, *Summa Iuris Canonici in Usum Scholarum Concinnata* (3 vols., Vols.I-II, 4 ed., Romae: Apud Aedes Universitatis Gregorianae, 1945), II, n. 10 (hereafter referred to as Cappello, *Summa Iuris Canonici*); Schaefer, *De Religiosis ad Norman Codicis Iuris Canonici* (3. ed., Romae: S.A.L.E.R., 1940), p. 221; Augustine, *A Commentary*, III, p. 104; also cf. Raus, *De Sacrae Obedientiae Virtute et Voto*, §42.

(19) Wernz-Vidal, *Ius Canonicum*, III, n. 126.

(20) Cf. Can. 196.

Canon 196 describes the power of jurisdiction principally from the aspect of its relation to the external and the internal forum, but the explicative words of the definition, *seu regiminis,* contain a clue to the extensive meaning of the power of jurisdiction as including legislative, judicial, and coercive authority. Jurisdiction is a power proper to a juridically perfect society, namely, the Church, and therefore comprises a legislative, a judicial, and a coercive power as distinct from the power of Orders.[21]

Authors endeavor to include all that the Code implies in Canon 196 by giving various explanatory definitions. Thus Chelodi (1880-1922), defined jurisdiction in general as a *potestas publica circa regimen aliorum,* and ecclesiastical *jurisdiction as a potestas publica regendi fideles in ordine ad salutem aeternam.*[22] From a careful comparison of Canon 196 with the definition given by Chelodi, it is apparent that the author omitted a very important factor, namely, the source of the power of jurisdiction, which is Christ, the Founder of the Church. His definition would have been more satisfactory had he included this element. Wernz-Vidal does this in the definition which he gives: "*Iurisdictio vero ecclesiastica est publica potestas regendi homines baptizatos in ordine ad sanctitatem et beatitudinem supernaturalem a Christo vel ab Ecclesia per iniunctionem sive missionem canonicam alicui concessa.*[23] In the definition, the author indicates the origin of ecclesiastical jurisdiction, namely, that it derives from Christ either directly or through the Church. True ecclesiastical jurisdiction never arises from the will of the people, as does civil jurisdiction in some instances, but must always be a participation in that

(21) Clancy, *The Local Religious Superior,* p. 4.

(22) *Ius de Personis iuxta Codicem Iuris Canonici, Praemisso Tractatu de Principiis et Fontibus I.C.* (2. ed. a Sac. Ernesto Bertagnolli, Tridenti: Libr. Edit. Tridentinum, 1927), n. 125 (hereafter referred to as Chelodi, *Ius de Personis.*)

(23) *Ius Canonicum, II, De Personis,* n. 48.

potestas regiminis which the Church has received from its Divine Founder.

Since the Church alone possesses this power essentially, it follows that the Church alone can confer this power upon others. The jurisdiction of the Church denotes an authority divinely bestowed primarily upon the Head of the Church, the Supreme Pontiff, and upon the Bishops and through them upon other rulers in the Church.

Distinctions between Jurisdiction and Dominative Power

From the foregoing, the differences between jurisdiction and dominative power may be summarized as follows:

a) *Origin:* Jurisdiction has been bestowed upon the Church by its Divine Founder; dominative power arises from the wills of the members of a juridically imperfect or subordinate society that exists within the perfect society, which is the Church.

b) *Nature:* Jurisdiction comprises legislative, judicial, and coercive authority; dominative power includes that power by which a Religious Superior governs the actions of his subjects to the attainment of the end of a particular Institute according to the Constitutions of the Institute.

c) *End:* Jurisdiction has been conferred upon the Church for the public good; dominative power has for its end primarily the good of the individual.

d) *Possession:* Jurisdiction, as it exists in the Church, is enjoyed by the Sovereign Pontiff and the Bishops in consequence simply of the office they hold, but by Superiors of Exempt Clerical Institutes as a result of concession; dominative power is possessed by all Religious Superiors alike.

Article 3. Vow of Obedience and the Promise of Obedience

From the foregoing preliminary notions it follows that there are pronounced differences between the vow of obedience as taken by members of Religious Institutes and the promise of obedience as made by secular priests at their ordination. To begin with, the special obligation of secular priests to obey their Ordinary emerges in the form of a promise to the ordaining prelate, and not, as in the case of Religious, in the form of a vow, which is made to God.[24]

A second difference and deriving from the natures of a promise and a vow, is the binding force of each. The vow of obedience made by members of Religious Institutes binds them through the virtue of religion; the promise made by secular priests obliges through the virtue of fidelity.[25]

The main difference between the vow of obedience as made by Religious and the promise as made by secular priests lies in the extent of the objects commanded. The vow of obedience extends to all those matters which a legitimate Superior may command "in virtue of the vow" according to the Constitutions and Rules of the Institute. The promise of obedience, on the other hand, extends simply to the limits that are set within the Code of Canon Law. In one sense, the power of the Bishop is more intensive, since he possesses jurisdictional power, i.e., legislative, judicial and coercive powers. In another sense, the power of the Religious Superior is more extensive, since

(24) Jone, *Commentarium in Codicem Iuris Canonici,* Vol. I (Paderborn: F. Schöningh, 1950), p. 136; Augustine, *A Commentary,* II, p. 73; Coronata, *Institutiones Iuris Canonici,* I, p. 189, n. 1.

(25) Vermeersch-Creusen, *Epitome Iuris Canonici* (6. ed., 3 vols., Mechlinae-Romae: H. Dessain, 1937-1946), I, 249; Coronata, *Institutiones Iuris Canonici, I, p.* 189, n. 1; Wernz-Vidal, *Ius Canonicum,* II, p. 93, n. III.

it extends to all phases of the subject's life, whereas the power of the Bishop pertains essentially to those phases which concern the government of the diocese.

Article 4. Origin of the Obligation of Canonical Obedience

Section 1. Incardination

The obligation of canonical obedience may arise in several different ways. The normal method of incurring this obligation is linked with incardination. Incardination denotes the affiliation of a secular cleric with a particular diocese. The process by which a lay person (for all practical purposes, a seminarian) becomes incardinated, or passes from the lay state into the clerical state, is first tonsure.[26] Usually a Bishop ordains his own subjects, intending him for the service of another determined diocese by agreement with the Bishop of that diocese, the candidate is immediately incardinated in the other diocese. The obligation of canonical obedience to the Bishop of the latter diocese arises *ipso facto,* i.e., immediately and automatically.[27]

In the event that a Bishop ordains his own subject, in tending him for the service of another diocese not yet determined, the cleric is incardinated by first tonsure in the diocese of the ordaining Bishop, but later can be transferred to another diocese by formal excardination and incardination.[28] There are still other methods of incardination under the various circumstances provided for in the Code of Canon Law, and in every instance, once a

(26) Can. 111, §2.

(27) Pontificia Commissio ad Codicis Canones Authentice Interpretandos, 17 aug. 1919; Bouscaren, *Canon Law Digest* (2 vols. and Supplement through 1948, Milwaukee: Bruce, 1934, 1943, 1949), I, p. 89 (hereafter referred to as *Digest*); *The Pontifical Commission for the Authentic Interpretation of the Code,* July 24, 1939; Digest, II, p. 52.

(28) Can. 969, §2.

cleric is validly incardinated in a diocese, the obligation of canonical obedience to the local Ordinary of the diocese in which he is incardinated arises *ipso facto.* The very affiliation of a cleric with a diocese by incardination necessarily imports the idea of a special obligation of obedience to the ecclesiastical Superior of that diocese or territory. By the very nature of his position therein, he must be subject permanently to a definite ecclesiastical Superior from the time of his first reception into the clerical state.(29)

Religious clerics are not incardinated by tonsure. Religious clerics by membership become affiliated with their Order or Congregation, but this relationship is designated not as an incardination, but rather as an enrollment *(adscriptio).* Candidates become canonically affiliated with their Institute when they make their profession of vows. From that moment on they become attached to the Institute in a permanent manner, so that they are no longer free to withdraw at will, and they become subject to a Religious Superior whose commands they must obey. Religious profession must precede induction into the clerical state by first tonsure, for Canon 567, §2, provides: "During the novitiate, novices may not be promoted to Orders (i.e., including first tonsure)." When a religious receives first tonsure, according to the opinion of Wernz-Vidal and McBride, he does not become incardinated in his own or in any other diocese, since it is not for their service that he is being promoted, but rather for the services of the Religious Institute to which he already belongs.(30)

(29) McBride, *Incardination and Excardination of Seculars,* The Catholic University of America Canon Law Studies, n. 145 (Washington, D. C.: The Catholic University of America Press, 1941), p. 287.

(30) *Ius Canonicum,* II, n. 59; *Incardination and Excardination of Seculars,* p. 298.

Section 2. Status of Voluntary Ex-Religious

An interesting and important question arises if a religious cleric should voluntarily leave a Religious Institute after the expiration of his temporary vows.

The Code of Canon Law provides for the instance in which a religious cleric in Major Orders voluntarily leaves an Institute, or is not allowed to make his profession, or is actually dismissed.[31] There does not seem to be a satisfactory solution for the instance in which a religious cleric in Minor Orders, or even a tonsured religious cleric, for that matter, voluntarily leaves his Order or Congregation after the expiration of his temporary vows. If he receives these Orders (or even tonsure) before he took his vows in religion, according to the unanimous opinion of the authors, he remains a cleric of the diocese to which he belonged before he joined the religious community.[32] The reason for this is apparent, since the cleric in question did not lose his diocese, since it is only by perpetual profession that a cleric automatically relinquishes his diocese.[33] But what about the case in which a candidate receives tonsure (and possibly Minor Orders) after his novitiate? If such a candidate for the priesthood should voluntarily leave the Religious Institute at the expiration of his temporary vows, what is his canonical status? The Code of Canon Law does not expressly treat this question. Nor do the authors offer any definite help in the matter. There are nearly as many opinions as there are authors. A few questions naturally arise: 1) Is such a person automatically reduced to the lay state? or does he remain

(31) Canons 637-643.

(32) Blat, *Commentarium Textus Codicis Iuris Canonici* (5 vols. in 6, Romae, 1919-1927), II, *De Religiosis,* p. 552; Schaefer, *De Religiosis,* p. 907, n. 1524; O'Neill, *The Dismissal of Religious in Temporary Vows,* The Catholic University of America Canon Law Studies, n. 166 (Washington, D. C.: The Catholic University of America Press, (1942), p. 179.

(33) Canons 115 and 585.

a cleric? 2) If he is reduced to the lay state automatically, how then is he re-instated in the clergy if he should proceed to Major Orders, since neither tonsure nor Minor Orders are ever repeated? 3) If he remains a cleric, is he an acephalous cleric? or is he automatically incardinated in the diocese that was his before he entered the Religious Institute?

Some authors maintain that such a cleric is automatically reduced to the lay state. They base their argument upon an analogy drawn from Canon 648.[34] The analogy, in the mind of the writer, seems to be unwarranted. It seems rather that such a cleric would not be automatically reduced to the lay state, for the reduction to the lay state spoken of in Canon 648 is in the nature of a penalty. But in penalties it is always the more benign interpretation that should be followed, in accord with Canon 2219, §1.

Reduction of a cleric in Minor Orders to the lay state is treated in Canon 211, §2. A cleric in Minor Orders is reduced to the lay state automatically for the reasons mentioned in the law, or upon his own volition with notice to the Ordinary, or through a decree of the Ordinary, for a just cause, namely, if upon mature consideration the Ordinary prudently judges that the cleric cannot be promoted to Sacred Orders with honor to the clerical state. The reasons for the automatic reduction of a cleric in Minor Orders to the lay state are accurately described in Canon Law. If a cleric in Minor Orders: 1) contracts marriage, Canon 132, §2; 2) volunteers for military service, Canon 136, §3; 3) in temporary vows is dismissed from the Religious Institute, Canon 648; 4) in perpetual vows is dismissed from the Religious Institute, Canon 669, §2, he is automatically reduced to the lay state. If the

[34] Leitner, *Handbuch des katholischen Kirchenrechts* (5 vols., Vol. III, *Das Ordensrecht,* 2. ed., Regensburg: Kösel und Pustet, 1922), III, p. 480; Schaefer, *De Religiosis,* p. 735.

legislator had wished to reduce a religious cleric, who *voluntarily* leaves his Religious Institute at the expiration of his temporary vows, to the lay state, he could have said so explicitly.

The second factor in the reduction of such a cleric to the lay state is his own volition, with notice to the Ordinary. This seems to imply that if such a person should desire to proceed to Major Orders, and has not manifested any intention whatsoever of abandoning the clerical state, he would remain a cleric.

The third factor is a decree on the part of the Ordinary that such a cleric is reduced to the lay state. Now, until such a decree has been issued, one would not be warranted in making the assertion that such a cleric is automatically reduced to the lay state.

The only logical conclusion, then, is that a person who has received tonsure and Minor Orders, or tonsure alone for that matter, after making temporary profession, and has left his Institute at the expiration of these vows, remains a cleric. This seems to be the opinion of the majority of the authors. However, very few authors will state their opinion in so many words. Schaefer (+1948), for instance, maintains that such a person remains an *"ecclesiastic"* and *"pertains"* to the diocese of his domicile. He does not state explicitly that he is a *"cleric"* and is *incardinated"* in the diocese of his domicile. It is difficult to explain his use of the word "ecclesiastic" in preference to the canonical term "cleric" or the word "pertinet" in preference to the canonical term of incardinated."[35] Chelodi was much more explicit, for he stated that such a person definitely remains a cleric. However, he also stated that such a person seems to have only the same juridical status as a layman. He further recognized the difficulty of the situation by asking the following questions: how is he to be incardinated should he desire

(35) Cf. Schaefer, *De Religiosis*, p. 907, n. 1525.

to proceed to Major Orders? by reception of the subdiaconate?[36]

Most of the authors consulted by the writer presuppose that such a person remains a cleric as long as he does not positively exclude himself from the clerical state by his own volition. Thus Woywod (1880-1941), held this opinion for he proposed the following question: "If he was promoted to Minor Orders in the community during his temporary vows, and then obtains a decree of secularization (*a fortiori,* if he should leave at the expiration of his vows) must his proper Bishop receive him as a cleric? He proceeded to answer this question: "It seems the Bishop must receive him, for the religious has not yet lost his proper diocese. Since, however, the Bishop has the right to judge who is and who is not a fit subject for the priesthood in his diocese, the Bishop may make use of the power which Canon 211 gives him, namely, for a just reason he may reduce the ex-religious to the lay state."[37] Toso shared the same view and so did Beste, Sweeney, and Schaaf (1883-1946).[38]

It is the opinion of the writer that such a person remains a cleric, but with the rights, privileges, and obligations of the clerical state suspended. This seems to be the only logical solution until his status is definitely established through a decree of the Bishop of his domicile, or through perpetual profession in another Religious Institute, or through the reception of Major Orders. Hence, in spite of the provisions of Canon 111, §2, such a person

(36) *Ius de Personis,* p. 189, n. 108.

(37) Woywod, *A Practical Commentary on the Code of Canon Law* (revised by Callistus Smith, revised and enlarged edition, 2 vols., New York: Jos. F. Wagner, Inc., 1948), I, n. 577.

(38) Toso, *Commentaria Minora* (5 vols. in 2, Romae: Marietti, 1920-1927), V, 234; Beste, *Introductio in Codicem,* p. 174; Sweeney, *The Reduction of Clerics to the Lay State,* The Catholic University of America Canon Law Studies, n. 223 (Washington, D. C.: The Catholic University of America Press, 1945), pp. 82-83; Schaaf, (Episcopus proprius ordinationis religiosorum"—*The Ecclesiastical Review,* XC (1934), 495.

must be classified as a "clericus acephalus." Canon 111, §2, provides for a permanent state, and thus there is no inconsistency in admitting that by way of a transitory duration a cleric may be unattached either to a diocese or a Religious Institute.

The question to be considered is whether such a person (an ex-religious in temporary vows, who has received tonsure [and Minor Orders] after his profession, but who has left the Institute *voluntarily* at the expiration of his temporary vows) is automatically incardinated in the diocese of his domicile which he had before taking his temporary vows.

The solution depends upon the part one has accepted in the foregoing controversy. Since the writer has accepted the part which recognizes such a person as remaining a cleric, it is altogether logical to endeavor to establish his canonical status.

As was stated above, the Code of Canon Law makes no explicit provision for the canonical status of such persons. Nor are the authors of much help in this matter either. Their opinions range from a positive statement that these persons are not incardinated to an implication that they are, at least in some cases, incardinated in the diocese which was their domicile before they entered Religion.

Chelodi stated that a cleric of an exempt Institute, if he leaves voluntarily at the expiration of his temporary vows, is not incardinated in any diocese, and thus seems to be an acephalous cleric.[39] However, he continued, if one has received tonsure before entering Religion, or if one enters a non-exempt Religious Institute with dimissorial letters from his Ordinary, he remains incardinated in his diocese up until the time of his perpetual profession.[40]

(39) *Ius de Personis*, n. 108, a).

(40) *Ius de Personis*, n. 108, a) footnote n. 2.

Other authors are much more noncommittal in their opinions. Thus Schaefer, when treating of this matter, stated that such a person remains an "ecclesiastic" and "pertains" or "belongs" to the diocese of his origin or domicile.[41] Schneider was apparently evading the issue in translating the term *"pertinet"* as "incorporated" or "incardinated" in this passage.[42] Schaaf did not say directly that such a cleric becomes automatically incardinated in the diocese which he had before he entered Religion, but he very strongly hinted at it. He argued in this manner: In virtue of Canon 585 such a cleric has not lost the diocese he had in the world. Hence, if he desires to continue in the clerical state, he must return to that diocese, and the local Ordinary is obliged to receive him. Schaaf drew this conclusion from an analogy with Canon 641, §1. This Canon, however, deals with clerics already constituted in Major Orders. He further argued that this was implied in a declaration issued by the Congregation of Bishops and Regulars, January 20, 1860: "Ad 4. Si professi votorum simplicium . . . per Apostolicam dispensationem ab emissis votis soluti fuerint, (Ordinarius) se gerat cum illis prout cum ceteris suis Dioecesanis sese gerere debet." If a cleric had made temporary profession and thereupon had received an apostolic dispensation from his vows, then the Bishop was to treat him as he would his own "Diocesans."[43]

Relative to this point, Beste very aptly makes a distinction between a cleric who had joined an exempt Institute and one who had joined a non-exempt Institute. He maintains that a religious who has joined an exempt Institute and therein has received tonsure (and Minor Orders)

(41) *De Religiosis,* n. 1525.

(42) Schneider, *Status of Secularized Ex-Religious Clerics,* The Catholic University of America Canon Law Studies, n. 284 (Washington, D. C.: The Catholic University of America Press, 1948), pp. 24-25.

(43) Bizzarri, *Collectanea in usum Secretariae Congregationis Episcoporum et Regularium edita* (2. ed., Romae, 1885), pp. 858-859.

after profession of temporary vows is not incardinated in any diocese, inasmuch as he was not promoted for the service of any particular diocese. Consequently, he logically concludes that such a cleric must seek a benevolent Bishop for incardination if he wishes to proceed to Major Orders.[44] It is a different matter if such a cleric had entered a non-exempt Institute and had received tonsure (and Minor Orders) therein. In this case he would be incardinated in the diocese of the Ordinary of the place, and consequently would have to return to this Ordinary, and the latter would have to receive him. At first sight it would almost seem that Beste, by the term, *Ordinarius loci,* refers to the Ordinary of the place where the non-exempt Religious Institute House is located. In this case he would be incardinated in the diocese of the Ordinary of the place, and consequently would have to return to this Ordinary, and the latter would have to receive him. This solution, in the mind of the writer, is not objective. In the first place, such a solution would impose too great a burden on the Bishop of the diocese in which the Religious House is located, for if this were the norm to be followed, the Ordinary of the place in which the Religious House is located would have to provide for each and every case in which members in temporary vows left the Institute, many of whom would not even have been members of his diocese before entering Religion.[45]

(44) *Introductio in Codicem,* p. 174, n. 3.

(45) *Introductio in Codicem,* p. 174, n. 4. A personal inquiry made of Dr. Beste, February 26, 1954 revealed his opinion on this matter: "We must distinguish: 1) There are non-exempt Institutes in which *by privilege* the superior himself can authorize the ordination of, or grant dimissorials to his subjects. If a religious thus ordained to tonsure or Minor Orders should leave after temporary vows, he has no claims against any Bishop, since no Bishop was in any way responsible for the ordination. Such a cleric will therefore have to find an *episcopus benevolus receptor* who will accept him and make him his subject and then in conformity with the law of canon 956 promote him to further Orders for his (the Bishop's) diocese. If he finds no such Bishop, he falls back into the lay

The proper Bishop for the conferral of tonsure and Minor Orders to non-exempt religious is the Bishop of the place where the candidate had his domicile before entering Religion.[46] The present arrangement whereby the Ordinary of the place in which the religious house is located confers tonsure and Minor Orders appears to be an arrangement of convenience. It would certainly cause quite a commotion if every Bishop of the subjects to be promoted to tonsure and Minor Orders had to be present for the ordination of a large class! This confusion is obviated by the local Ordinary's conferral of tonsure and Minor Orders with the proper dismissorials from the proper Bishops of the candidates.

A decision of the Sacred Congregation for Bishops and Regulars on January 20, 1905, brought out two points: 1) that members of non-exempt societies may not be ordained without dismissorial letters of their proper Bishops; and 2) that they always belong to the diocese which they had as their proper diocese before they joined the society.[47]

A practical inference to be drawn from this is that Bishops should exercise more circumspection in the issu-

state, as one may conclude from canon 211, §2. 2) If the superior of the Religious Institute, to which the ordinand belongs, has no such privilege, the ordination of the subject is governed by the law of seculars (canon 964). In other words, such a candidate falls under the law of canon 956 and must seek Orders from the *episcopus proprius (cum vel sine origine)*. Who is the *episcopus proprius* in that case? This is debatable, cf. Beste, p. 519 under Canon 964, n. 2. One may conclude as follows: Whoever (of the two Bishops in question) actually ordained or granted the dimissorials, the same will also be the *episcopus proprius* to whom the ordained cleric belongs. If this Bishop does not want to assume further responsibility, he can excardinate the ordinand; if no Bishop can be found who will accept the cleric, he falls back into the lay state as was said above under the first point."

(46) Schaaf, "Episcopus proprius ordinationis religiosorum,"—*The Ecclesiastical Review*, XC, (1934), 504.

(47) *S.C. Ep. et Reg.*, 27 ian., 1905—*Acta Sancta Sedis*, XXXVIII (1905), 11-13.

ance of dimissorial letters. Charity, if not justice, should prompt a diligent issuance of such dimissorial letters. As much diligence should be exercised in issuing the dimissorial letters for religious candidates as is exercised in the promotion of a Bishop's own diocesan candidates to tonsure and Minor Orders.

It is quite a different matter in the case of exempt religious. It does not seem fair that a Bishop should become burdened with ex-religious clerics in Minor Orders to whom dimissorials were granted by their own higher Religious Superiors apart from all knowledge and consent on the part of the local Ordinary of the candidate. The problem is not as formidable as it appears on the surface, for the privilege to grant dimissorial letters is given to the Religious Superiors by the Sovereign Pontiff, to whose supreme authority the Bishop is likewise subject. Likewise the burden imposed upon a diocese is not as great as it is made out to be, for often the ex-religious cleric will of his own volition reduce himself to the lay state. But if he desires to continue in the clerical state and presents himself as a cleric in Minor Orders, three courses are open to the Bishop: 1) he can permit the secularized cleric to remain in the ranks of the diocesan clergy as a secular cleric; 2) he can excardinate him if another Bishop is found who is ready to incardinate him according to Canons 112-117; or 3) he can reduce him to the lay state if the conditions warrant it, according to Canon 211, §2.[48]

In the mind of the writer, this question is far from settled, and one may with good reason hope for a decision in this matter from the Pontifical Commission for the Authentic Interpretation of the Code. In the meantime, a practical settlement of this problem has been promulgated in a joint decree of the Sacred Congregation of Religious and the Sacred Congregation of Seminaries and

(48) Schneider, *Status of Secularized Ex-Religious Clerics*, p. 29.

Universities on July 25, 1941. This decree states that a person who has by any title belonged to a religious family is not to be admitted to a seminary, before the Ordinary has had recourse to the Sacred Congregation of Seminaries and Universities, which after all is said and done, will inform the Ordinary of its judgment in the case.[49]

As far as the obligation of respect and obedience is concerned for an ex-religious cleric who has hopes of proceeding to Major Orders in the secular clergy, it is rather a matter of prudence than of justice. For instance, if the Bishop should make any precepts concerning the diocesan clergy, especially those of a prohibitive nature, it would be rash for such a cleric to disregard them as not applying to him. In a word, such a cleric would act wisely to observe all the diocesan statutes regarding secular clerics.

Article 5. Special Obligation of Priests

Priests are singled out in Canon 127 for this special obligation of respect and obedience. Both secular and religious priests are included in this canon. The obligation incumbent upon all clerics in general is solemnly enhanced in the form of a public profession by the newly ordained priest towards the very end of the ordination ceremony. Immediately before the last blessing of the Ordination Mass, the ordaining Bishop, holding the hands of the newly ordained priest within his own, asks of him: "Do you promise me and my successors reverence and obedience?" The priest answers; "I do promise." [50] Speaking of this promise made by all priests on the occasion of their ordination to the sacred priesthood, Pope Benedict XIV pointed out the gravity of this promise of reverence and obedience: "Accordingly we do not regard this solemn promise of reverence and obedience as

(49) *AAS.*, XXXIII (1941), 371.

(50) *Pontificale Romanum*, tit. *de ordinatione presbyteri.*

an unenforceable and empty formula."[51]

The underlying reason for this special obligation on the part of priests is obvious, for all priests, secular or religious, co-operate much more closely and more frequently with the Ordinary in the administration of the affairs of the Church and the care of souls than do clerics of a lower rank.

Article 6. The term "Ordinary" in Canon 127

Canon 127 states that all clerics, especially priests, have the obligation to respect and obey their own Ordinary. Reverence is due to all ecclesiastical superiors either on the basis of their position through the reception of Orders or through the wielding of jurisdiction, and hence this canon implies no new obligation. The obligation of clerical obedience, as stressed in this canon, implies a special obligation apart from the general obligation on the part of all the Ordinary's subjects. The important word in this canon is the word "own" with reference to the Ordinary. This word defines the extent of the cleric's obedience in regard to the person who commands this obedience. A cleric or a priest is not bound to obey any Bishop other than his own, as long as he remains within his own diocese. If a cleric or a priest should leave his own diocese, he would be bound to obey the laws affecting the public good of the territories or dioceses through which he travels.[52] Since the promulgation of the Code of Canon Law, the Sacred Congregation of the Council has issued two letters which deal with priests living outside their own dioceses. The first letter dealt with the matter of priests on vacation outside their own diocese and the regulations were as follows:

1. Priests who for health's sake desire to leave their dio-

(51) Ep. *Ex quo,* 14 ian. 1747, §11—*Fontes,* n. 374; *supra,* p. 39.

(52) Canon 14, §2.

ceses for any length of time must submissively ask this permission of their Ordinary, informing him at the same time of the date of their projected departure and return, and of the places to which they desire to go.

2. The Ordinaries shall take care to consider and weigh with discrimination the reasons which the priests allege in asking for permission to leave the diocese; they shall carefully consider beforehand the character and way of life of those who ask the permission, and shall grant it only with due caution.

3. They shall, moreover, require that their priests always chose such hotels and stopping-places as are not unbecoming to ministers of God.

4. The Ordinaries shall, besides, report the names of these priests as soon as possible to the Curia of the diocese to which they go, and shall state the amount of time that has been allowed them, and the hotel or house in which they are to stay.

5. The priests, too, when they arrive at the place where they wish to stay, shall as soon as possible present themselves at the Curia of that place, or, according to the circumstances, call upon the rural dean or at least on the pastor, who shall thereupon report the matter to his Ordinary.

6. (a) Ordinaries of places to which priests are accustomed to go for health's sake shall carefully and attentively keep watch over the priests who are staying there, either personally or through priests whom they shall have specially assigned to this task; and they shall not allow the visiting priests to perform sacred functions unless they obey the above prescriptions.

(b) In order the more readily to hold these priests to their duty, they shall establish suitable penalties which they shall incur if they give scandal, or if in any way they do anything that is unworthy of the priestly character.

(c) They may also threaten them with suspension to be incurred *ipso facto* in case they attend public theaters, "movies," revues, or other profane shows of the kind, or if they lay aside their clerical dress.

(d) Finally, they shall actually inflict upon these ecclesiastics, penalties in accord with the sacred canons, if they fail to obey these prescriptions and the other laws of the Church.

(e) They shall carefully report the matter to the proper Curia of the priests concerned, and if need be, also to this Sacred Congregation.

7. In this matter, Ordinaries shall be watchful even as regards religious; they shall decree penalties against them according to the sacred canons in case they misbehave, and report them to their major Superiors.[53]

With reference to the above cited regulation 6. (c) Donovan has treated the matter of movies, especially as obtaining in the United States as America, quite intelligently and fairly: "The motion picture has become an integral and influential factor of modern life. Nowhere is this truer than in the United States. Among the four million who daily enter American motion picture theaters, there are to be numbered many clerics and priests. In itself the motion picture is either a great instrument for good or a powerful weapon for evil. . . . This is the attitude of the Church toward motion pictures. It is easy to understand that the laws of the Church do not forbid motion pictures in themselves, but forbid clerics and priests to attend such motion pictures as are objectionable or unbecoming." [54]

The second letter concerns priests teaching in public schools. This letter contained the following legislation:

(53) *Digest,* I, 138-140.

(54) Donovan, *The Clerical Obligations of Canons* 138 and 140, The Catholic University of America Canon Law Studies, n. 272 (Washington, D. C.: The Catholic University of America Press, 1948), pp. 161-164.

1. The prescriptions of the Holy See regarding clerics and priests who are attending universities or so-called normal schools remain in effect; especially those which are contained in a Letter of the Secretary of State, of 20 Nov., 1920, are to be exactly observed.

2. Priests, even after they have obtained the master's degree, *remain as before assigned to the service of their respective dioceses, and subject to their respective Ordinaries.*

3. The Ordinaries should see to it that these priests take up the work of teaching in their diocese, especially in sacred seminaries of clerics, or in private schools.

4. A priest shall not seek or accept such a position in the public schools without the explicit consent of his Ordinary; and this consent is by its nature revocable.

5. The Ordinary is gravely bound in conscience not to give his consent except in the case of those who excel in piety and learning, and who will give good example both privately and publicly to the students and the other professors.

6. The Ordinary may permit one of his priests to go to another diocese for the purpose of taking a position as teacher, *but on condition that the position be held subject to the will of his own Ordinary and of the Ordinary of the place.* Accordingly, *the priest is bound to obey without pretext* of excuse, both his own Ordinary, if he calls him back for the service of the diocese, and the Ordinary of the place if he orders him to leave.

7. The Ordinary shall not permit a priest of his diocese to teach in another diocese without having previously notified the Ordinary of the place and obtained his permission.

8. A priest who is about to take up the work of teaching in another diocese, shall without delay call upon the

Ordinary of the place, whom, according to c. 94, *he must regard as his own Ordinary as long as he remains in that place,* and to whose watchfulness, authority, and correction he must submit.

9. The Ordinary of the place can:

a) For just cause, to be reckoned at his prudent discretion, order that the preists be assigned to some church;

b) Arrange that the priest be under the special watchfulness of the rural dean, the pastor, or some other priest;

c) Require the priest to report in what house he habitually lives, and with what persons; forbid him to have in the same house with him or to associate in any way with women who might be the occasion of suspicion; order him, if the Ordinary deems it necessary or advisable, to live in some religious house to be designated by the Ordinary;

d) Forbid him to teach in schools for girls only, or for both girls and boys; and to teach or tutor girls privately;

e) Command him to observe each and all of the common obligations of clerics; especially to attend the meetings or conferences for the solution of cases in moral and liturgy; to help the pastor of the place in religious teaching of children; on days of obligation, to give a brief explanation of the Gospel or of some chapter of Christian doctrine at the Mass which he celebrates for the people;

f) Admonish, correct, and, if need be, punish with suitable penalties according to the sacred canons, a priest who departs from the straight path.

10. The Ordinary of the place shall, at the expiration of each scholastic year, report to the Ordinary of the priest on his life and conduct.

11. A priest professor who wishes to leave the place for any considerable time must notify the Ordinary of the place; when he begins his summer vacation, he should

pay him a visit of obedience; and when he returns to his own diocese, he must present himself to his Ordinary and faithfully obey his orders.[55]

Relative to this matter the Sacred Consistory issued a decree concerning clerics attending secular universities. The last three items of this decree are particularly apropos to the subject of canonical obedience. They are as follows:

3. Priests so attending secular universities are not thereby exempt from the examinations which are prescribed in canons 130 and 590; on the contrary, they should be the more strictly required to undergo them, lest through interest in profane sciences they neglect ecclesiastical studies, contrary to the prescriptions of c. 129.

4. After finishing their studies in any secular university, the *priests remain subject to their Ordinary in exactly the same way as before,* and *they remain bound to the service of the diocese.* Hence, no one of them has the right to accept at will a professorship or other office, especially against the wishes of his Ordinary. If anyone does so, let him be punished by suitable penalties, not excluding suspension.

5. All of this applies *congrua congruis referendo,* to religious, and even to regulars.[56]

Section 1. Ordinaries in general

The Code of Canon Law enumerates the various Ordinaries in Canon 198, §1. They are: 1) The Roman Pontiff for the whole world; 2) within his respective territory, the residential Bishop; 3) the Vicar General of the dio-

[55] *AAS,* XIX (1927), 99-100; Translation taken from Bouscaren's *Digest,* I, 116-118.

[56] *AAS,* X (1918), 238; Translation taken from Bouscaren's *Digest,* I, 115.

cese;[57] 4) the Abbot and the Prelate *nullius* within their territories; 5) the Vicar General of an Abbot or a Prelate *nullius;* 6) the Administrator Apostolic; [58] 7) the Vicar Apostolic; 8) the Prefect Apostolic; 9) all those who in default of any of these succeed temporarily to the government, either according to law or by virtue of approved constitutions, and 10) Major Superiors for their own subjects in clerical exempt Religious Institutes.

Whereas canonical obedience is due the residential Bishop, that is, the Bishop who has actual jurisdiction over the whole diocese, it is not due the auxiliary or the coadjutor Bishop, unless he be also the Vicar General in the diocese wherein he is appointed to serve.

Section 2. The Vicar General

The question of canonical obedience to the Vicar General cannot be gainsaid, for he has, by virtue of his office, jurisdiction over the entire diocese in spiritual and temporal matters. His jurisdiction, however, is limited to the extent of the Bishop's own ordinary jurisdiction, except in those affairs which the Bishop has reserved to himself, or which by law require a special mandate from the Bishop.[59] The Vicar General must take care not to use his powers contrary to the mind and will of the Bishop.[60]

An apparent difficulty arises if the Vicar General should issue a command directly and manifestly contrary to the mind and customary practice of the Bishop. In such an instance, which course should a priest follow, the command of the Vicar General? or the mind and practice of the Bishop? It may very easily occur that the Vicar General may not have been informed of some pend-

(57) Canon 366, §1.
(58) Canons 312-315.
(59) Canon 368, §1.
(60) Canon 369, §2.

ing transaction, which, for example, the Bishop may have discussed with the chancellor or a pastor. The course of action to be followed is not too difficult to decide. a) If the matter is not urgent, the chancellor or pastor can explain the situation to the Vicar General in the hope that the Vicar General will change his own command to agree with that of the Bishop, or delay the execution of the issue until the Bishop decides the matter. b) If the matter is urgent, but the Bishop can be contacted by telephone or telegraph, the matter can be amicably settled to the satisfaction of all concerned. c) If the matter is urgent and the Bishop cannot be contacted by telephone or telegraph (for instance, the Bishop is on his *ad limina* visit to Rome, or is on his vacation), then, after the situation has been explained to the Vicar General and if the latter persists in enforcing his command, the chancellor or pastor should abide by the decision of the Vicar General. In doubt, the presumption favors the Vicar General.[61] It is advisable that the Vicar General's command be obtained in writing.

Section 3. Temporary Ordinaries

The Code of Canon Law has provided for the government of territories or dioceses by temporary Ordinaries in extraordinary circumstances. These temporary Ordinaries are mentioned in 9) above. For the sake of completeness these eventualities will be listed:

1) In the case of an episcopal see vacant on the account of death, resignation, or transfer of a Bishop, the government of the diocese devolves upon the Cathedral Chapter (or on the Diocesan Consultors in those dioceses where there are no Chapters), unless an Apostolic Administrator has been appointed by the Holy See.[62] During this

(61) Chelodi, *Ius de Personis*, p. 198, n. 115.

(62) Canon 431.

short period of time (eight days at most according to Canon 432) the ordinary jurisdiction of the Bishop in temporal and spiritual affairs devolves upon the Chapter or Diocesan Consultors as a body. Hence during this time the obligation of canonical obedience obtains for whatever decrees these bodies may issue.

2) Within eight days from the notice of the vacancy of the episcopal see, the Cathedral Chapter (or the Diocesan Consultors in those countries which have no Chapter) must elect a Vicar Capitular (or correspondingly a Diocesan Administrator) for the government of the diocese. Once he has made the profession of faith before the Chapter or the Diocesan Consultors, as he is required to do in Canons 1406-1408, he immediately obtains the rightful exercise of jurisdiction over the diocese.[63] Hence all clerics, especially priests, must obey the Vicar Capitular or the Diocesan Administrator, unless he evidently transgresses his powers in violation of Canon 435.

3) If the Bishop is banished, captured, exiled or otherwise incapacitated so that he cannot communicate even by letter with the people of his diocese, the government of the diocese, unless the Holy See has provided otherwise, shall rest either with the Vicar General, or with another priest delegated by the Bishop.[64] The case provided for here is far from being an imaginary one; it has occurred repeatedly within the first half of this century in Mexico, Poland, Germany, and Russia.

4) A further special provision is made in Canon 429, §5, for the rare case in which the Bishop is under excommunication, interdict, or suspension. In this event, the Vicar General's jurisdiction is likewise suspended together with that of the Bishop.[65] In such a case the

(63) Canon 438.
(64) Canon 429, §1.
(65) Canon 371.

Archbishop—or if the Archbishop is likewise under censure, or fails to act, then the oldest suffragan Bishop shall have recourse to the Holy See at once, through which provision will be made for the government of the diocese. The one appointed by the Holy See as Administrator will possess jurisdiction over the diocese, and hence the obligation of canonical obedience will be directed toward this temporary administrator.

Scholion

The writer feels that the subject of Ordinaries has been amply treated in this dissertation, henceforth when the term "Ordinary" is used in this dissertation, any or all the persons mentioned in Canon 198, §1, are meant, with the exception of Major Superiors in Exempt Clerical Religious Institutes.

Since what applies to a Bishop in his diocese in the matter of canonical obedience is equally applicable to all the above mentioned Ordinaries in their respective territories, the discussion will henceforth be limited to the canonical obedience which is due to a residential Bishop.

Clerics of Religious Institutes are bound to obey their particular Superiors in virtue of the vow of obedience, and since their mode of life is provided for in the rules and constitutions of their respective Institutes, it will not be the aim of this study to treat this aspect of obedience. The main purpose of this work will be to show the relationship between the Ordinary of the diocese and the secular priests in whatever capacity they may serve in the care of souls or in the administration of the diocese. Religious clerics and priests will henceforth be treated only in so far as they come under the jurisdiction of the residential Bishop.

CHAPTER IV

THE BASIS OF THE OBLIGATION OF CANONICAL OBEDIENCE

The basis of the obligation of canonical obedience on the part of clerics, and especially of priests, is unquestionably the fact that the Ordinary or the Bishop has been entrusted with the government of the Church in his particular territory or diocese. Residential Bishops rule their respective dioceses with *ordinary* power, but under the authority of the Sovereign Pontiff.[1] From this it follows that residential Bishops are not merely governors delegated to oversee the administration of their specific dioceses, but, in the truest sense of the word, are rulers in their own right. Their power is *ordinary* because it flows from the very nature of the episcopate, or from the episcopal office, which has been formally, i.e., as such in it essential features, instituted by Christ.[2]

It is quite intelligible and necessary that the power of the Bishop should be subject to him who possesses exclusively and fully the primacy in the universal Church, *viz.*, the Sovereign Pontiff. This subjection to the authority of the Supreme Pontiff is expressed through the election, ratification or confirmation of the Bishop-elect by the Apostolic See; through his consecration, which is reserved to the Apostolic See; through the account he must periodically render to the Holy See concerning the government of the diocese entrusted to his care; and through his recourse to the Apostolic See for those extraordinary permissions and dispensations which are not given him in virtue of his office but which have been reserved to the Apostolic See.

(1) Canon 329.

(2) Augustine, *Rights and Duties of Ordinaries* (St. Louis, Missouri: Herder, 1924) p. 3.

Within these defined limitations, the residential Bishop is the true ruler of his diocese. His is the right and the duty in both spiritual and temporal matters to govern the territory or diocese entrusted to him with the legislative, judicial, and executive power to be exercised according to the norms of the Code of Canon Law.(3)

Article 1. The Legislative Power of the Bishop

A residential Bishop has the power to enact any law for his diocese, provided that it is not contrary to the common law of the Church, (4) to particular laws issued by the Holy See for the territory subject to him, or to the laws of a plenary or a provincial council. Though a residential Bishop cannot make laws contrary to the common law, he can make laws in accordance with it *(secundum ius commune)* or in extension of it *(praeter ius commune)*.(5)

Section 1. Synodal Legislation

The Bishop's legislation according to the law *(secundum ius)* consists in specifically determining, according to the peculiarities of his diocese those matters which the higher law merely generically regulates without further determination as to their particular applications, or which are explicitly left to the Bishop for more accurate regulation.(6) The most common form of episcopal legis-

(3) Canon 335, §1.

(4) Supremum Signaturae Apostolicae Tribunal, *Romana* (Iurium), 15 dec. 1923—*AAS,* XVI (1924), 106-107.

(5) Wernz-Vidal, *Ius Canonicum,* II, 746-747; Chelodi, *Ius de Personis,* p. 310, n. 3; Beste, *Introductio in Codicem,* p. 270; Coronata, *Institutiones,* I, n. 394; "Der kanonische Gehorsam," *Archiv für katholisches Kirchenrecht,* LXXXII (1902), 304.

(6) Donnelly, *The Diocesan Synod,* The Catholic University of America Canon Law Studies, n. 74 (Washington, D. C.: The Catholic University

lation is to be found in the diocesan synodal statutes. The primary purpose of the diocesan synod is the consideration and adoption of local laws. The Code of Canon Law constitutes an orderly and complete arrangement of the present universal law of the Church; the diocesan statutes should form a supplement to the Code. The peculiar conditions of each diocese created by geographical location, difference in civil laws, territorial customs, the advance in scientific discoveries, as well as the fluctuating attitude of social convention, demand a specific application of the universal law. Within proper limits, the Bishop, after consultation with members of the synod, can adopt whatever he deems not only necessary but also useful for the welfare of either the clergy or the laity of his diocese.[7] In both these instances the laws enacted, as true laws, oblige in conscience.[8]

The chief subject matter of the synodal statutes lies within those things which are termed as being beyond the law *(praeter legem).* Herein are included many points about which, because of varying conditions, the Code of Canon Law, or plenary or provincial decrees have made no provision, but which call for a decision in order that priests in the ministry be enabled to do their work properly. Questions concerning which there is a controversy among canonists as to whether or not provisions have been made in the general law of the Church likewise would be included in the Bishop's legislative powers, for the Bishop is the *authoritative,* not the *authentic,* interpreter of Canon Law within his diocese.[9]

of America, 1932) p. 87; "Der kanonische Gehorsam," *Archiv für katholisches Kirchenrehht,* LXXXII (1902), 307.

(7) Donnelly, *The Diocesan Synod,* p. 88.

(8) It is not within the scope of this work to endeavor to determine the culpability of the infraction of episcopal legislation. That lies within the realm of Moral Theology.

(9) Cf. *infra,* p. 97.

Section 2. Extra-Synodal Legislation and Precepts

In addition to the diocesan synodal statutes, extra-synodal laws and precepts may be enacted by the Bishop in the exercise of his legislative power. An extra-synodal law is simply what the term implies, a law issued by the legislator outside of the diocesan synod. Provided that the object of such a law lies within the scope of the Bishop's legislative powers, and complies with all the necessary requirements of the promulgation of laws in general, it constitutes a true law, and hence its binding force is the same as that of any true legislation.

A precept is an order emanating from the competent authority to individuals or to a community in a particular case. A precept is an order, and therefore, it is not to be confused with a mere exhortation, a counsel, or an admonition. Accordingly it possesses the same binding force as a law, especially if it is a jurisdictional precept.[10]

In canonical matters every ecclesiastical legislator is empowered to issue precepts. Consequently, all who have jurisdictional power, ordinary or delegated, in the external forum, can issue precepts.[11]

Precepts given to individuals bind them wherever they go, but they cannot be juridically enforced, and they cease with the expiration of the authority of the one who imposed them, unless they were issued in the form of a legal document or before two witnesses.[12]

Unquestionably, a cleric or a priest must obey a valid precept given to him individually, and unless limiting clauses are attached to it, the precept is presumed to be

(10) Coronata, *Institutiones,* I, n. 31, 1° a; Cicognani, *Canon Law* authorized English version by J. O'Hara and F. Brennan (Philadelphia: Dolphin Press, 1934), p. 636.

(11) The Vicar General likewise may issue precepts, though he has administrative power only.—Cicognani, *Canon Law,* p. 636.

(12) Canon 24.

personal rather than territorial.[13] Precepts given to a group are regarded by Michiels in two ways: either as given to the members as individuals, or as given to the community as a group. When the precept is given to the members as individuals, it is equivalent to a singular precept given to each member. When it is given to the members as a group, then, if the group is one which is capable of receiving a law, and if there is attached to the precept a definite degree of stability, for all practical purposes, such a precept is equivalent to a law.[14] The obligation to obey a precept, whether given to an individual or to one as a member of a group, e.g., of the diocesan clergy, is beyond dispute.

Section 3. Restriction of Episcopal Legislative Power

The legislative power of the Bishop must be exercised according to the norms of the sacred canons as provided in canon 335, §1. Hence the legislative power of the Bishop cannot touch matters which are outside his competence. Thus only the Holy See can institute irregularities which bar the lawful reception of Orders, or impeding and diriment matrimonial impediments, or feast days and days of fast and abstinence.[15] Likewise a Bishop cannot legislate in matters which the Code has reserved to the provincial council or the provincial gathering of Bishops, e.g., the determination of the cathedraticum or other taxes.[16] By the same token a Bishop cannot interfere with what the higher law expressly and undoubtedly per-

(13) Wernz-Vidal, *Ius Canonicum* II, 196, (III).

(14) *Normae Generales Juris Canonici* (2 vols., Lublin: Universitas Catholica, 1929), I, 519; Wernz-Vidal, *Ius Canonicum,* I, *Normae Generales* (2. ed., Romae, 1952), I, 197, (III).

(15) Canons 1038, §2; 1244, §1, §2. The Ordinary of the place is permitted to announce feast days and days of fast and abstinence *per modum actus,* but he may not ordain that this regulation continue on a habitual or permanent basis. Canon 1244, §2.

(16) Canons 1504; 1507, §1; 1909, §1.

mits by attempting to repeal or forbid the use of a permission granted by it or to impose an obligation incompatible with it.[17] It must be noted, however, that the legislation of a subordinate legislator is without legal force only if the higher law is certainly binding. If there is doubt of law, the Bishop is not forbidden to make a contrary enactment according to the principle of canon 15, *"Leges in dubio iuris non urgent."* A subordinate legislator may consider it as non-existent and proceed to enact his own law until an authentic interpretation has been given to the contrary.

It must likewise be noted that the powers of the Bishop are thus restricted when the higher law expressly and undoubtedly grants a permission or privilege. Inasmuch as the higher law may fail to prohibit some act, it does not follow that a legal permission has been granted. Such a grant is made only when there exists a positive declaration that the legal permission has been established. Accordingly a law which only doubtfully grants a permission cannot be considered as forbidding or ruling out a contrary law enacted by a subordinate legislator. The permission must be expressly and certainly stated in law.[18] A legal permission is granted in law either through the positive concession of a right of the legal capacity to perform a certain act, or through the allowance to perform an act which is not essentially evil, or finally through the granting of legal immunity to an act which is not intrinsically wrong. Each of these possibilities will be explored in relation to the obligation of canonical obedience.

The right to interpose an appeal or a recourse in accord

(17) Chelodi, *Ius de Personis,* p. 310; Wernz-Vidal, *Ius Canonicum,* II, p. 746, n. 599.

(18) Wernz-Vidal, *Ius Canonicum,* II, p. 599; Ryan, *Principles of Episcopal Jurisdiction,* The Catholic University of America Canon Law Studies, n. 120 (Washington, D. C.: The Catholic University of America Press, 1939), p. 134.

with the principles enunciated in Canon Law is a definite and certain right granted by the Code of Canon Law. Hence a Bishop cannot by law or precept or in any other way impugn a cleric's or a priest's option to make use of this right. Since the right to interpose an appeal or a recourse is an express and certain right granted unequivocally by the Code, a priest is neither disobedient nor irreverent in exercising this right and in enjoying the consequent liberties.

Recourse implies the exercise of a person's right to defend himself against probable or possible injustice or injury. Every man has the right to protect himself against probable and possible violation of any of his rights. Every complete legal system, both civil and ecclesiastical, has included remedies to be used by members of society against the possible judicial and extrajudicial violation of their rights.

In Canon Law *appeal* is the ordinary means available against such possible violations through sentences pronounced by judicial authorities in Church government.[19]

Recourse is the remedy established by positive ecclesiastical law against the extrajudicial acts, decrees, ordinations, dispositions, decisions and transactions of superiors and against elections and the extrajudicial decisions of judges. The word *"recursus"* and its derivatives have no strictly specialized meaning in the Code. In one canon the word is used in the sense of a supplication,[20] such as may be made by a person who feels that he is being treated unfairly by a judge. In other places, recourse signifies the direction of a petition to a competent superior for his mandates concerning a censure which was absolved when the penitent was in danger of death, or in some very urgent case, by a priest who under ordinary circumstances would have lacked the power to grant the absolu-

(19) Can. 1879.
(20) Can. 1569, §2.

tion.[21] In still other canons various forms of the verb "recurrere" are used in the meaning simply of an approach to a superior.[22] Finally, the term "recourse" denotes a remedy or a means of redress against the extrajudicial acts of a superior.[23]

Fundamentally, every use of this word in the Code contemplates a subject's approach to someone constituted in authority. In the present work the term "recourse" is used in the meaning of a juridical remedy, or of a juridical means of redress. It may be defined as a plea made to a competent superior with a view to its possible unfavorable reflected upon the extrajudicial acts of a lesser superior, inasmuch as the one who presents the plea either claims or at least thinks that he has suffered injury in his rights or detriment to his status.[24] The purpose of this remedy is to obtain the correction or the revocation of the acts of the lesser superior.

Recourse is not always concerned with a strict right. In many cases it is indeed concerned with the violation of strict rights, such as that of a pastor to retain his parish.[25] However, many recourses deal with the interest or the concern of the party, rather than the strict right. No pastor has a strict right to be licensed to preach; yet when the Ordinary revokes this license, recourse may be made.[26] Consequently, one may say that recourse is concerned both with the rights and the interests of subjects. Recourse is based on justice and equity. A pastor who has been removed from office makes his re-

(21) Can. 2254, §2.

(22) Canons 48, §3; 81; 429, §5; 521, §2; 583, 2°; 2334, 2°.

(23) Canons 192, §3; 296, §2; 298; 345; 454, §5; 498; 513, §2; 647, §2, 4°; 699, §1; 880, §2; 970; 1340, §3; 1395, §2; 1428, §3; 1465, §1; 1601; 1709, §3; 1710; 1805; 2146, §1; 2153, §1; 2194; 2243, §§1 & 2; 2287.

(24) Roberti, *De Delictis et Poenis*, Vol. I (ed. altera, Romae: Libraria Pontificii Instituti Utriusque Iuris, 1938), n. 288; Beste, *Introductio in Codicem*, p. 791.

(25) Can. 2146.

(26) Can. 1340, §3.

course to the Holy See,[27] in order that he may be reinstated in his parish, and he seeks this reinstatement not as a favor from the Holy See, but as a matter of justice.

From what has preceded it is apparent that recourse differs in several points from judicial appeal. Recourse may be made from many kinds of actions, while appeal may be made from a definitive sentence only.[28] Appeal must be made within ten days of the notification of the publication of the sentence,[29] but a similar limited duration of time is generally not set as an imperative or essential condition for the making of a recourse. Appeal may be made orally,[30] while recourse must always be made in writing.[31] Appeal must always be made before the judge of the court from which the plea is carried to a higher tribunal *(iudex a quo)*.[32] Usually recourse does not suspend the decree, act, precept, disposition, etc., against which it is made, while an appeal is usually *in suspensivo*.[33] In practically every case recourse is made to the Holy See,[34] but appeal is *usually* made from the tribunal of a suffragan to that of the metropolitan.[35]

Article 2. The Judicial Power of the Bishop

The residential Bishop is by native right the proper ordinary judge of the first instance,[36] in all ecclesiastical

(27) Can. 2146, §1.

(28) Canons 1879; 1880.

(29) Can. 1881.

(30) Can. 1882, §1.

(31) Wernz-Vidal, *Ius Canonicum,* V, 527, footnote 125.

(32) Can. 1881.

(33) Can. 1889, §2.

(34) The exceptions are listed in cans. 162, §2; 1610, §3; 1709, §3; 1710; 2153, §1.

(35) McClunn, *Administrative Recourse,* The Catholic University of America Canon Law Studies, n. 240 (Washington, D. C.: The Catholic University of America Press, 1946), p. 15.

(36) Canon 1572, §1.

causes,[37] which by reason of any of the various recognized titles pertain to his diocese and are not reserved to the higher authority of the Roman Pontiff. His judicial competence is proportionate to his legislative competence, in the sense that he may function not only according to but also beyond the higher law. He judges according to the higher law those matters which have been regulated by the diocesan law, whether these diocesan laws themselves are according to or beyond the higher law.

The same principles which govern the cleric or the priest as to respect for and obedience to the Bishop as the diocesan lawgiver apply likewise as to the diocesan judge.

Article 3. The Executive Power of the Bishop

The Bishop's legislative and judicial power culminates in and is perfected by his executive power. This is the ultimate stage of diocesan government to which the legislative and judicial powers are directed, and without which the purpose of the Bishop's government of the diocese could not be attained. The executive power of the Bishop is proportionate to his legislative and judicial powers, that is, its force is not restricted to the common law, but may proceed beyond that law.

The first office of the Bishop's executive power is to insist upon the exact observance of the common law. This principle is very clearly enunciated in canon 336, §1, and is explained in §2 of the same canon. The Bishop functions with his executive power outside the law of the Code when he applies and enforces the particular diocesan laws established either by himself or by his predecessors in office. In some instances, for example in canon 2368, the superior law has specified norms to be followed in the application of the higher law. These of course the Bishop must follow. Likewise the Bishop may not dispense his

(37) Canon 1553.

subjects from the provisions of the higher law, except and in so far as this is permitted him by the higher legislator.[38] On the other hand, laws promulgated by the Bishop or by his predecessors in office depend for their application and enforcement upon the judgment of the Bishop.

It is not within the scope of this work to enumerate all of the possibilities in which a Bishop must execute a penalty in compliance with the higher law. One example will illustrate this principle. If it is conclusively proved that a priest is guilty of the crime of solicitation as listed in canon 904, he shall be suspended from the celebration of Mass and from the hearing of sacramental confessions, and if the gravity of his offense demands, he shall be declared disqualified for the hearing of confessions. He shall also be deprived of all benefices and dignities, of the active and passive voice in ecclesiastical elections, and be declared disqualified for all these, and in the more serious cases he shall be punished with degradation.[39] Thus it is not left to the Bishop's discretion to suspend or not to suspend such a priest from the celebration of Mass and the hearing of sacramental confessions. He shall also be deprived of his benefices and dignities, and of the active and passive voice in ecclesiastical elections. The canon does allow the Bishop to use his judgment in the matter of intensifying the penalty if the circumstances warrant it, by declaring such a priest disqualified for the hearing of confessions, and in the more serious cases by instituting the process for his degradation.[40]

In regard to diocesan laws, however, he can dispense

(38) Canon 81.

(39) Canon 2368, §1.

(40) An Instruction from the Sacred Congregation of the Holy Office, Rome, June 9, 1922, was sent to all the Ordinaries indicating the measures to be taken in the event that such a case should arise. This Instruction stipulated that this document was to be retained in the Diocesan Chancery archives, and that its contents be not divulged in any manner. The writer respectfully refers the Ordinary's attention to this document.

with their application or even abrogate the same, as often as in his own judgment such a relaxation or repeal of the law is more conducive to the spiritual welfare of his subjects.

The Bishop, within the limits of the positive higher law, remains the supreme executive official in the diocese. As such, therefore, he authoritatively directs the clergy not only in their private lives as Christians but also in their official public lives as well.[41]

The tremendous power granted to the Bishop in canon 2222, §1, very clearly indicates the mind of the higher lawgiver relative to the Bishop as the supreme executive official in the diocese. In virtue of this canon, the residential Bishop may punish the transgression of a law with a just penalty, even when no specific penalty was attached by law, if the scandal given or the special gravity of the violation demands it. He may resort to this expedient even without a previous threatening of the penalty. Ordinarily no penalty is to be inflicted for any violation of the divine or the ecclesiastical law, if the law does not decree a penalty. The normal procedure is that the offender is first to be warned and threatened with a penalty, and only then, if he disregards the warning and the threat can proceedings for the inflicting of the penalty be instituted. While the very wording of canon 2222, §1, clearly indicates that this power is to be used by the Bishop not indiscriminately, but only when the emergence of serious scandal or the special gravity of the violation of a law requires it, it also indicates that the higher legislator has granted the Bishop all the executive power necessary for the enforcement of the higher law and the effective administration of his diocese in extreme and serious cases.[42]

(41) Ryan, *Principles of Episcopal Jurisdiction*, pp. 141-143.

(42) While the canon uses the generic term "legitimate Superior," it is beyond doubt that the residential Bishop is included. An earlier canon, expressly excludes the Vicar General, unless he enjoys a special mandate in this regard.—Canon 2220, 2.

In laws to which a penal sanction is attached, the law itself serves as a warning, and if such a law is violated, proceedings for punishment may be opened immediately. The formalities of the criminal procedure must be observed according to canons 1933-1959. Since the spiritual welfare of the Church demands the reparation of scandal and an atonement for serious misconduct, the law grants to legitimate ecclesiastical superiors—foremost among whom must be included the residential Bishop—the authority to take immediate action in case of such scandal or misconduct.

Article 4. The Bishop as Authoritative Teacher and Administrator

In virtue of his position as ruler of the diocese, the Bishop enjoys two other offices which are necessary corollaries of the gubernatorial power which he possesses, namely, he is the authoritative teacher and administrator of the diocese. After treating the threefold power of the Bishop, one should also briefly consider his rôle of authoritative teacher and administrator.

The predominant idea contained in canon 335 is that it is the Bishop's duty and right to govern his diocese. This power extends to everything that is specifically diocesan. The purpose of a diocese is, in the final analysis, the salvation of souls. For this purpose the same means must be employed within the diocese as are used in the Church at large, namely, the teaching of Christian truth and the governing of the faithful according to that doctrine. The Bishop, therefore, in his jurisdictional capacity must be empowered to execute both these functions; he must be both the teacher and the ruler of his diocese.

The Bishop is the authentic and divinely appointed teacher of faith and morals within his diocese. Although individually or when assembled in particular councils the Bishops do not possess infallibility in their teaching, they are truly doctors and teachers of the faithful committed to their care, under the authority of the Roman Pontiff.[43] In virtue of his office, the Bishop is obliged to teach the Catholic faith within his diocese, and does so authoritatively.[44]

It is the Bishop who is the divinely appointed public teacher of his people. Others in the diocese may be more brilliant, more profound, more eloquent, more widely read theologians, more commanding personalities but it is from the Bishop that these latter receive their power to teach and in whose office they participate. Others in his diocese can teach publicly only insofar as he permits or calls them to assist him in his labors.[45]

Although it is quite possible that an individual Bishop may err in what he teaches, since he is not personally infallible, the mere possibility of error in a teacher does not exempt anyone from the duty of believing. In the rare case in which a Bishop should teach something which is known to be, or at least is suspected to be, at variance with the admitted doctrine of the Church, assent may, and in the former case must, be withheld. In the ordinary circumstances where no grave reason for doubt presents itself, his subjects should accept his doctrine, for he and he alone is the divinely appointed teacher of the diocese. His religious teaching has a claim upon his flock, which no other teaching, save the infallible teaching of the Church, can possibly have.[46]

From this one may logically deduce that the Bishop is the *authoritative* teacher and guardian of Canon Law within his diocese. It is his duty and right to interpret

(43) Canon 1326.

(44) Leo XIII, ep. encycl., *Sapientiae christianae,* 10 ian. 1890, n. 8,—*Fontes,* n. 605.

(45) Canon 1327, §2.

(46) Ryan, *Principles of Episcopal Jurisdiction,* pp. 79-83.

those points of Canon Law which have been passed over in silence, left undetermined, or treated in a generic manner.[47] The Bishop is not the *authentic* interpreter of the Code of Canon Law, not even for his own diocese. The prerogative of an authentic interpretation of the Canon Law is reserved to the supreme lawgiver, the Sovereign Pontiff, and those to whom this power has been delegated, e.g., the Pontifical Commission for the Authentic Interpretation of the Code.[48]

The Bishop's interpretation is neither absolute nor infallible. Hence the seeking of redress on the part of his subjects, clergy or laity, is admissible. Any interpretation made by a lower legislator, though it be authoritative, leaves available the remedy of recourse, just as the enactment of laws by an Ordinary offers the same possibility.[49] This is clearly stated in the Constitution *Romanos Pontifices* of Pope Leo XIII of May 8, 1881. "An authoritative interpretation of synodal law when made by Bishops as the heads of Synods—(but this is equally true with reference to the laws enacted by them outside the Synod)—has precisely the same force as the decrees themselves." Now, since redress can be sought against the decrees, it can also be undertaken against the authoritative interpretation which the Bishop may have issued.

The government of a diocese involves the need not only of a authoritative presentation of Catholic doctrine and principle, but also of an equally authoritative direction and guidance of the faithful according to doctrinal truth and in the application of these principles to conduct their daily lives. In this regard, each Bishop in his diocese, but under certain well-defined limitations, is to his flock

(47) Beste, *Introductio in Codicem,* p. 183, n. 2; Augustine, *Rights and Duties of Ordinaries,* p. 88.

(48) Augustine, *op. cit.,* pp. 90-91.

(49) Cicognani, *Canon Law,* p. 602.

what the Sovereign Pontiff is to the Universal Church.[50]

Within these well-defined limitations the authority of the Church is in his hands to exercise. In virtue of the authority inherent in the office which he holds, the Bishop is not merely a nominal head of the diocese but the real sovereign over it. He disposes concerning the participation of others in the ecclesiastical authority of the diocese and authoritatively directs its use.[51] The Bishop's prerogative to regulate authoritatively whatever is specifically diocesan is beyond dispute. This prerogative, however, reflects not simply a theoretical principle; rather, it consists in a concrete application of power for regulating the conduct and discipline of his subjects. By the very nature of his position as head of the diocese, it is his duty to apply the doctrine and principles of the Catholic faith to the practical aspects of the lives of his subjects, both clergy and laity.

Foremost among the objects subject to the administrative power of the Bishop is the supreme direction of the clergy. He has the right to keep a priest in his diocese, if he has entrusted him with certain ecclesiastical functions or an ecclesiastical position and has given him fitting means of support.[52] As often and as long as, in the judgment of their own Ordinary, the needs of the Church require it, clerics, unless they are lawfully excused by some impediment, must accept and faithfully execute the duty which has been entrusted to them by the Bishop.[53] Another object which is subject to the Bishop's gubernatorial power is that of the administration of ecclesiastical property. No alienation whatsoever of ecclesias-

(50) Bouix, *Tractatus de Episcopo, ubi et de Synodo Dioecesana* (2. ed., 2 vols., Parisiis, 1859), II, 100.

(51) Ryan, *Principles of Episcopal Jurisdiction*, pp. 83-84.

(52) Claeys-Bouúaert, *De Canonica Cleri Saecularis Obedientia*, pp. 200-204.

(53) Canon 128.

tical goods is possible without his consent, and he exercises supreme supervision over their administration.[54]

Closely connected with this is the Bishop's duty and right to supervise all matters relating to divine worship, to the administration of the Sacraments, to liturgical books, processions, Holy Mass, exorcisms, etc. His consent is necessary for the erection of churches and oratories. But in all these matters his power is not unlimited, for he must always conform to the enactments embodied in the Code of Canon Law.[55]

(54) Canons 1541, §3; 1532, §2, §3.

(55) Canons 1259-1306.

CHAPTER V

THE EXTENT OF THE OBLIGATION OF CANONICAL OBEDIENCE

Article 1. Positive Obligations of Clerics

Clerics are bound, above all things, to obey the Bishop in regard to those canons which treat of clerical discipline and the dignity of the clerical state. These are in the main to be found in canons 108 through 144. As was pointed out above, it is the Bishop's prerogative to interpret these canons according to the needs of his particular diocese. Hence, the Bishop has not only the right, but also the duty, to see that all clerics within his diocese frequent the Sacrament of Penance, devote some time daily to mental prayer, visit the Blessed Sacrament, recite the rosary, and examine their consciences.[1] The Bishop likewise determines the time and place for the secular priests' retreat, and without the express permission of the Bishop they may not absent themselves from it, except in a particular case and for a just cause. The Bishop is the judge concerning the validity of the excusing cause.[2] He determines also the procedure for the junior clergy examinations and the subject matter for the clergy conferences.[3] It belongs to the Bishop to decide whether living in the same house or habitually associating with certain women, even such as ordinarily are not under suspicion, may in particular cases be an occasion of scandal, or a danger to chastity,—and it is his, and not the cleric's, place to determine whether such cohabitation or association may be tolerated or should be forbid-

(1) Canon 125.

(2) Canon 126.

(3) Canons 130 and 131, §1.

den.[4] The decision regarding the propriety of the co-habitation or association belongs in all cases entirely to the Bishop, even when by normal standards the woman is above suspicion.

It is the prerogative of the Bishop to see to it that his clerics wear the clerical dress in accord with legitimate local custom and whatever regulations he may make in this respect.[5] Without consultation with the Bishop clerics may not go bail even on the security of their own property.[6] Without the permission of the Bishop, clerics may not undertake the administration of property which belongs to lay persons, nor may they assume secular offices which involve the duty of rendering an account, nor may they exercise the office of procurator or attorney in civil court, unless they do so in a case involving themselves or their church.[7] In those countries where the Holy See itself has not forbidden the holding of certain civil offices, clerics may neither seek nor accept civil offices without the permission of their own Bishop as well as that of the Bishop of the place where the election is to be held.[8]

Without the permission of the Bishop, clerics may not volunteer for military service, even though they undertake this as a means of becoming freed from compulsory service the sooner. The violation of this provision by a cleric in Minor Orders effects automatically his reduction to the lay state.[9]

Clerics may not absent themselves from their diocese for a notable time without at least the presumed permission of their Bishop.[10] Clerics who have obtained a leave of absence with the permission of their Bishop and

(4) Canon 133, §3.
(5) Canon 136, §1, §3.
(6) Canon 137.
(7) Canon 139, §3.
(8) Canon 139, §4.
(9) Canon 141, §1, §2.
(10) Canon 143.

have gone into another diocese may be recalled for a just reason, provided the laws of equity are observed. This is the right of the Bishop, since the absent cleric remains incardinated in his diocese. Hence, it follows logically that the cleric must obey, since he remains subject to the Bishop in whose diocese he is incardinated.[11] A Decree of the Sacred Congregation of the Council, 22 February, 1927 concerning priests teaching in Public Schools is quite apropos to this matter, particularly provisions, 6-9.

"6. The Ordinary may permit one of his priests to go to another diocese for the purpose of taking a position as teacher, but on the condition that the position be held subject to the will of his own Ordinary and the Ordinary of the place. Accordingly, the priest is bound to obey without pretext of excuse, both his own Ordinary, if he calls him back for the service of the diocese, and the Ordinary of the place if he orders him to leave.

7. The Ordinary shall not permit a priest of his diocese to teach in another diocese without having previously notified the Ordinary of the place and obtained his permission.

8. A priest who is about to take up the work of teaching in another diocese shall without delay call upon the Ordinary of the place, whom, according to c. 94, he must regard as his own Ordinary as long as he remains in that place, and to whose watchfulness, authority, and correction he must submit.

9. The Ordinary of the place can:

a) For just cause, to be reckoned at his prudent discretion, order that the priest be assigned to some church;

(11) Canon 144.

b) Arrange that the priest be under the special watchfulness of the rural dean, the pastor, or some other priest;

c) Require the priest to report in what house he habitually lives and with what persons; . . . order him, if the Ordinary deems it necessary or advisable, to live in some religious house to be designated by the Ordinary;

d) Forbid him to teach in schools for girls only or for both girls and boys; and to teach or tutor girls privately;

e) Command him to observe each and all of the common obligation of clerics; especially to attend the meetings or conferences for the solution of cases in moral and liturgy; to help the pastor of the place in the religious teaching of children; on days of obligation, to give a brief explanation of the Gospel or of some chapter of Christian doctrine at the Mass which he celebrates for the people;

f) Admonish, correct, and, if need be, punish with suitable penalties according to the sacred canons, a priest who departs from the straight path." [12]

No cleric may attend a secular university except at the request or with the approval of his Bishop. This is clearly deducible from the prescriptions of the Code; but it was the object of a decree of the Sacred Consistorial Congregation, issued April 30, 1918. Paragraph four of this decree clearly indicates that the obligation of obedience and respect on the part of clerics is a permanent duty.

"4. After finishing their studies in any secular university, the priests remain subject to their Ordinary

[12] *AAS*, XIX (1927), 99-100; Translation taken from Bouscaren's *Digest*, I, 117-118.

in exactly the same way as before, and they remain bound to the service of the diocese. Hence, no one of them has the right to accept at will a professorship or other office, especially against the wishes of his Ordinary. If anyone does so, let him be punished by suitable penalties, not excluding suspension." [13]

Perhaps the most important canon relative to canonical obedience is to be found in canon 128, which stipulates that as often as and as long as, in the judgment of the Bishop, the needs of the Church require it, clerics must accept and faithfully execute any office which shall be entrusted to them by the Bishop, unless they are lawfully excused in view of some impediment. Clerical employments are divided into ordinary and extraordinary, in view of the law and the custom obtaining in various places. Ordinary duties or employments may be imposed even apart from their necessity, provided they are useful for the good of the Church in the judgment of the Bishop. Extraordinary employments can be imposed only when they are necessary; but the decision regarding their necessity rests with the Bishop.[14] The judgment not only regarding the necessity of the Church, but also concerning the validity of the alleged impediment pertains to the Bishop and not to the cleric.[15] Hence, if a priest receives a notification of a future appointment to some ecclesiastical office or position for which he feels unqualified or in regard to which he feels incapable of fulfilling all the duties conscientiously, he may honestly offer his excusing reasons to the Bishop, but it remains for the Bishop to make the final decision.[16] If the Bishop

(13) *AAS,* X (1918), 238; Translation taken from Bouscaren's *Digest,* I, 115.

(14) Bouscaren-Ellis, *Canon Law,* p. 108.

(15) Coronata, *Institutiones Iuris Canonici,* I, 189.

(16) "Der kanonische Gehorsam," *Archiv für katholisches Kirchenrecht,* LXXXII (1902), 294; Haring, *Grundzüge des katholischen Kirchenrechts,* I, p. 213, n. 3.

should reject the excuse, the priest must obey by accepting the appointment. The responsibility for the success or failure in this appointment, provided that the cleric endeavors faithfully to fulfill it, is on the Bishop's conscience.

This canon (128), in the mind of the writer, is the determining factor in the canonical transfer of pastors (canons 2162-2167). Provided the Bishop has complied with the other canons treating of the transfer of pastors (2162-2165), a pastor must accede to the wishes of the Bishop.[17] Unless the Bishop's action is evidently unfair, a priest should accede to his wishes. If the pastor feels that the transfer is unfair, recourse to the Holy See against the transfer is permissible in accord with the principle laid down in canon 2146, but this recourse is not advisable unless the Bishop's action is evidently unfair.[18] It is neither a manifestation of disobedience nor an indication of disrespect if a pastor who feels that his removal or transfer is unjust in any way, avails himself of this right. This is an instance wherein a certain and unequivocal right has been granted to pastors by the Code. The pastor who has instituted a recourse must inform the Bishop that he has done so; furthermore, in obedience to the Bishop's decree he must leave the parish.[19] When such a recourse has been interposed, all the acts of the process must be forwarded to the Holy See, and with the outcome of the recourse pending, the Bishop cannot validly assign the parish in question permanently to any other priest.[20]

The obedience required by canon 127 is determined by the natural and the positive divine laws, by the principles

(17) Canon 2166.

(18) Vermeersch-Creusen, *Epitome Iuris Canonici,* III, 363.

(19) S.C.C., *Romana et Aliarum* (de fatalibus ad recurrendum), 12 ian. 1924—*AAS,* XVI (1924), 162-165.

(20) Canon 2146, §2, §3.

of Canon Law, by the legislation of the Plenary and Provincial Councils, and by the statutes of the Diocesan Synod.

The object and extent of canonical obedience is determined, on the one hand, by the clerical state and office, and, on the other, by the measure of the Bishop's jurisdiction. The Bishop is thereby entitled to enforce the common law, which governs the clerical state and office in general (canons 124-144). Over and above the obligations enunciated in these canons, clerics are bound to obey every law or command of the Bishop, as long as it remains within the limits of his jurisdiction, in so far as the law or command corresponds with the spirit of the Church's law or, at any rate, does not contradict it. Canonical obedience, in a word, includes whatever is lawfully imposed by precept, even beyond the common law, for the good of the Church.(21)

Article 2. Restrictions on Bishop's Preceptive Power

Canonical obedience, however, cannot be urged outside of the proper canonical limits. A cleric can never be obliged to do anything prohibited by the natural or the positive divine laws. It is almost inconceivable that a Bishop would ever issue a command contrary to the natural or positive divine laws. If, however, such a command were given, a cleric would not only be allowed to disregard such a command, but rather would be bound in conscience to abstract from it. In so doing, it is evident, a cleric would not be violating canon 127.(22)

(21) Haring, *Grundzüge des katholischen Kirchenrechts*, I, p. 213, n. 3; Augustine, *A Commentary*, II, 72; "Der kanonische Gehorsam," *Archiv für katholisches Kirchenrecht*, LXXXII (1902), 312; Beste, *Introductio in Codicem*, p. 183; Jone, *Commentarium in Codicem Iuris Canonici*, I, 136; Chelodi, *Ius de Personis*, p. 198; Vermeersch-Creusen, *Epitome Iuris Canonici*, I, 218.

(22) Reiffenstuel, Lib. I, tit. XXXIII, n. 19.

Likewise, a Bishop cannot command anything prohibited by Canon Law.[23]

The Code of Canon Law specifically lists one such prohibition: "Should one who is ordained refuse to receive higher Orders, he can not be forced by the Bishop to receive them," (Canon 973, §2). The Church demands that the candidates for the clerical state be absolutely free in offering their lives to the service of God and the Church. In order to insure this absolute freedom on the part of clerics in the pursuit of their vocation, the Church has leveled a sanction of excommunication against anyone, of whatever dignity, who in any manner forces a man to embrace the clerical state.[24] It matters not whether this force or grave fear be direct or indirect or be occasioned through fraud, deceit, threats, verbal contentions, or even inopportune pleading. The words *"of whatever dignity,"* clearly indicate that Bishops are not exempt from incurring this excommunication.

While canon 2352 speaks of forcing one to *enter* the clerical state, there seems to be doubt whether this sanction likewise includes those who force a cleric in any manner to receive *higher* Orders. Canon 973, §2 clearly indicates that a cleric who does not desire to receive higher Orders is perfectly free to refuse to accept them.

The Bishop's right to command obedience is likewise restricted by the rights unequivocably granted to clerics by the Code of Canon Law.[25] Thus the functions reserved to pastors (canon 462), the personal right of the pastor to the stole fees (canon 463, §1), the option in the transfer of Manual Masses (canon 838), the right of every

(23) Jone qualifies this principle and inserts the clause, *"nisi a lege ecclesiastica dispensare possit."—Commentarium in Codicem Iuris Canonici,* I, 136.

(24) Canon 2352.

(25) Chelodi, *Ius de Personis,* p. 198; Jone, *Commentarium in Codicem Iuris Canonici,* I, 136; Beste, *Introductio in Codicem,* p. 183; Bouscaren-Ellis, *Canon Law,* p. 108.

priest to hear the confessions of a person in danger of death (canon 882), the right of approved confessors to hear confessions while on an ocean voyage (canon 883),[26] outlined in canon 2254, cannot be revoked or tampered with in any way by the Bishop, unless he has a special indult. Thus, unless a Bishop possesses a special indult, he cannot validly issue a law or a regulation within the Diocesan Synod or outside of it whereby pastors would be obliged to turn in to the Chancery all or any stole fees, for this is clearly a violation of canon 463.

The same is true concerning the disposal of Mass stipends, as was clearly indicated by a resolution of the Sacred Congregation of the Council, on February 21, 1921.[27] A law of a pre-Code Provincial Council had forbidden the transfer of Mass stipends outside the diocese without the permission of the Ordinary. After the promulgation of the Code, the question arose whether this law remained in effect or was revoked in accord with canon 6, 1°, as being contrary to canon 838. The *animadversiones* of this case are apropos at this point:

> "The legislative power of Bishops does not extend to passing laws contrary to the general law of the Church, though they may further define what is left undefined by the general law. It follows that Bishops cannot by their laws prohibit what is expressly and clearly permitted by the general law, unless the general law gives them the power! (Wernz, *Ius Decretalium,* II, n. 756)"

This principle applies as well to the laws of a Provincial Council, for these are episcopal laws. The approval of the Holy See, though required merely as

(26) This privilege has been extended to priests travelling by air—Pius XII, motu propr., *"De facultate audiendi,"* 16 dec. 1947—*AAS,* XL (1948), 17.

(27) *AAS,* (XIII) 1921, 228-230.

a condition of legitimate promulgation (cf. cans. 290, 291), does not give them specific papal authority.

Canon 838 clearly gives priests the right to transfer Masses, even outside the diocese, without the permission of the Ordinary of the sender. This freedom was deliberately intended, because the prudent sending of Mass stipends is a form of charity and a help to poor priests and churches in need of it. Canon 838 applies, however, only to Masses of which the priests have the free disposal." [28]

There is an amazing and discouraging divergence of classification and terminology among the authors concerning matters which are not directly connected with the government of the diocese and which inherently are not objects of clerical obedience. Thus, the authors consulted by the writer list the following as categories in which the cleric ordinarily is not subject to the Bishop's commands: civil, political, private, temporal, and indifferent matters.[29] For the sake of clarity, the writer proposes the following classification:

civil	Political non-political
personal (private)	spiritual temporal (indifferent)

In civil matters that are purely political, a cleric enjoys all the liberty granted by the law of the land. Thus a cleric may belong to any political party he wishes,

(28) *AAS,* XIII (1921), 228-230; Translation taken from Bouscaren's *Digest,* I, 399-400.

(29) Beste, *Introductio in Codicem,* p. 183, n. 3; Chelodi, *Ius de Personis,* p. 198, n. 115; Ramstein, *Manual of Canon Law,* p. 176; Cappello, *Summa Iuris Canonici,* I, n. 229; Jone, *Commentarium in Codicem Iuris Canonici,* I, 136; Berutti, *Institutiones,* II, 120; Prümmer, *Manuale Iuris Canonici* (Friburgi Brisgoviae, Herder, 1928), p. 90.

provided, of course, that such a party is not openly condemned by the Church, e.g., the Communist party. Hence, in this country, a cleric may freely espouse the Democratic or the Republican party or platform according to his conscience.

Another political right which a cleric enjoys is the right to vote. A cleric may use or refrain from using his right to vote according to his own free volition. There may be occasions when a Bishop may very strongly urge his subjects to make use of their right to vote. This was the case in the last few years when the Holy Father exhorted every Catholic and Religious to vote in order to defeat the Communist party in Italy. This may well be construed as a reminder of their duty flowing from the positive divine law. From this, however, it does not follow that a Bishop can command his clerics to vote for a particular political candidate for the simple reason that he is a Catholic. Unless a political candidate is an avowed enemy of the Church, other things being equal, a cleric may vote for whomsoever he pleases.[30]

The same principle applies to those civil matters which are non-political. As long as these matters do not entail a harmful influence upon the Church's government and advancement, they are not in and of themselves the object of canonical obedience. In particular cases they may for incidental reasons become objects of episcopal jurisdiction. For example, a priest is perfectly free to join the Civil Defense Unit. If, however, in a particular case the Bishop foresees that the priest's activity therein will consume too much of the time that he should be dedicating to his pastoral work, the Bishop is fully within his right to forbid such a priest to continue in this pursuit.

Ordinarily, personal (private) matters are not subject to episcopal legislation. Personal or private matters may

(30) Schneider, "Der kanonische Gehorsam," *Archiv für katholisches Kirchenrecht* LXXXII (1902), 315.

be of the spiritual or the temporal order. In the spiritual sphere, in particular cases, and if the circumstances warrant it, these personal or private matters may possibly become the objects of canonical obedience by way of a warranted particular precept. Inasmuch as the Code of Canon Law does not determine the time of a cleric's meditation, or of his recitation of the rosary or of the Divine Office, a cleric is at perfect liberty to arrange for the fulfillment of these duties at any time of the day that will suit his schedule. If abuses crept in, a Bishop would be within his jurisdiction to take measures to correct such a situation. This ordinarily would be remedied by means of a particular precept rather than by way of general legislation.

Personal or private matters of a temporal nature likewise are ordinarily left to the discretion and prudent judgment of the individual cleric. Under normal circumstances the following are not fit objects of episcopal jurisdiction; the arrangement of furniture in a priest's private study, innocent hobbies, such as stamp-collecting, pursuit of one of the natural sciences, development of a musical talent, etc. The personal finances of a cleric, the disposition of his last will and testament and matters relating to his inheritance or to other personal transactions are not ordinarily fit subjects for legislation on the part of the Bishop. If a priest is squandering his finances or incurring debt by irresponsibly living above his means, a Bishop could correct such a cleric by means of a particular precept. The same principle can be applied to all the other examples cited—only when they are abused and thereby harm or injure the good of the Church, should the Bishop take steps to remedy the situation, and then preferably by a particular precept rather than by general legislation. In the absence of abuse, a priest is perfectly free to trade at any store he pleases, to purchase whatever make of automobile he judges most satisfactory for his work, to take out insurance with the company which offers him the best protection for the lowest premiums, etc. A priest cannot validly be forced to join any diocesan insurance program if he chooses not to do so.

An apparent abuse of episcopal power consists in a regulation whereby moral force is exerted on clerics before Ordination in order to constrain them to take a pledge to abstain from alcoholic beverages for a determined period of time after their Ordination. In spite of attestations that this pledge is taken voluntarily, in reality it amounts to an alternative "or else." In the final analysis this unjust infringement on human liberties is in at least some cases tantamount to the creation of a new impediment to Holy Orders, which of course stands expressly contrary to the ruling enacted in canon 983.

A much disputed point may profitably be considered at this juncture, namely, may a Bishop enact legislation whereby assistant priests are forbidden to possess automobiles? The main contention which favors the positive point of view is that their possession of automobiles is not conducive to the common good. In the opinion of the writer, this contention seems ill-founded in view of the fact that times have changed from the days of the original enactment of this legislation. Nowadays, in this country, automobiles are hardly to be considered a luxury. On the contrary, an assistant pastor's priestly work is frequently seriously hampered by the lack of transportation facilities, especially in rural and suburban parishes. The writer is well aware that abuses are possible, but while abuses are indeed to be eradicated, in most instances this can be provided for by means of particular precepts. There was a time when clerics were forbidden to ride bicycles, because they were considered dangerous and were at the same time regarded as savoring of luxury and sport! [31]

(31) Schneider, "Der kanonische Gehorsam," *Archiv für katholisches Kirchenrecht*, LXXXII (1902), 310; Jone, *Commentarium in Codicem Iuris Canonici*, I, 126.

On the supposition that in a particular diocese there is no legislation that bans the possession of an automobile, the next question arises: May a Bishop legislate upon the make or class of automobile a priest may own? Provided a priest has the means to purchase and maintain an automobile, the choice of the type or make should rather be left to the prudent judgment of the individual priest, for after all it is his own personal investment. Obviously, if a priest were to incur a sizable debt in consequence of which his priestly work would be seriously hindered, a Bishop would certainly have the right to intervene in the matter, if need be, by way of a particular precept. But, in the mind of the writer, it seems to be an abuse of the Bishop's power to issue a law through which all priests would be held to purchasing only specified makes of automobiles or be limited to selecting a certain class or remaining within a fixed price range.

Article 3. Penal Sanctions Against Irreverence and Disobedience

The Code of Canon Law contains two canons in particular which prescribe the punishment to be meted out to those (clerics included) who fail to show the proper respect for clerics of a higher order. Persons who lay violent hands on the person of a . . . Bishop, automatically incur excommunication reserved in a special manner to the Apostolic See.[32] Any person who in public periodicals, speeches, or pamphlets, has injured (i.e. calumniated) either directly or indirectly . . . his own proper Ordinary, or who has excited animosity or hatred against his acts, decrees, decisions or sentences, shall be compelled by the Ordinary even with censures to make satisfaction, and shall be punished with appropriate penalties and penances in proportion to the gravity of his guilt and

(32) Canon 2343, §3.

the necessity of repairing the scandal.[33] The injuries spoken of in this canon include all offensive, insulting remarks, all slander and revelations of secret faults or defects, and finally all agitation against the official actions of the above-mentioned ecclesiastical authorities. One author does not hesitate to state that even private criticism may under certain circumstances be equivalent to public injury and, hence, the Ordinary could proceed against the instigator of such undermining of ecclesiastical authority.[34]

Whereas canon 127 does not contain a penal sanction, that sanction is invoked through canon 2331, §1 and §2. This latter canon adopts the jurisprudence of the 17th and 18th centuries, in so far as it authorizes Bishops to punish insubordinate clerics, even with censures, in proportion to their crimes.[35] While the first paragraph of canon 2331 does not specifically mention clerics, it undoubtedly includes them in an eminent degree. Any person (*a fortiori,* a cleric) who stubbornly refuses to obey the legitimate precepts of the Roman Pontiff, or his proper Ordinary, shall be punished with appropriate penalties, not exclusive of censures, in proportion to the gravity of their contracted guilt. Paragraph two of canon 2331 mentions clerics specifically, and clearly indicates the penalties that are to be inflicted upon those who conspire against the authority of . . . their own Ordinary, or against their legitimate commands, and also upon those who provoke subjects to disobedience; if the provoking agents be clerics, they shall be deprived of their dignities, their

(33) Canon 2344.

(34) Private conversation injurious to the person or office of the said dignitaries is not mentioned in canon 2344, but, if through the often-repeated guilty conversation such talk becomes public, the Ordinary has the right to proceed against such persons, even though their offense does not fall under the terms of canon 2344—"public periodicals, speeches or pamphlets"—Woywod, II, p. 542.

(35) *Supra*, p. 37.

benefices, and also other offices; if they be religious, they shall be deprived of their office and also of the active and passive voice in canonical elections.[36]

If, for the purpose of hindering the exercise of ecclesiastical jurisdiction, a pastor shall dare to stir up the populace, to promote public subscriptions in his favor, to excite the people by speeches or writings, or take other similar actions, he shall be punished at the discretion of the Ordinary with penalties proportioned to his guilt, and, if necessary, even with suspension.[37] This canon deals with the case of removal of a pastor from his parish. The Code of Canon Law has provided the norms to be followed in the removal of a pastor, and the means of defense which may be adopted by a pastor who believes himself unjustly treated. If a pastor stirs up the people of the parish and induces them to resist the orders of the local Ordinary, he is guilty of disobedience to the ecclesiastical authority, even though his removal was unjust. For the sake of the public welfare, the Church forbids him to employ the means of defense condemned in canon 2337, §1.

Likewise if any priest arouses the people to prevent a pastor or administrator legitimately appointed by the local Ordinary from taking possession of his office, the priest is guilty of interference with the exercise of ecclesiastical jurisdiction and makes himself liable for severe punishments.[38]

Article 4. Qualities of Canonical Obedience

The obedience which a secular cleric must show his Bishop is not without limit, nor is it a blind or absolute obedience whereby the cleric is reduced to the status of a "yes-man" or an ecclesiastical puppet. In fact, canon

(36) Wernz-Vidal, *Ius Canonicum,* VII, nn. 444-445.

(37) Canon 2337, §1.

(38) Canon 2337, §2.

425 explicitly states that those who are appointed to serve in the capacity of Diocesan Consultors must take an oath to perform their duties, foremost among which is to advise the Bishop to the best interests of the diocese, without respect for persons. There may arise circumstances where a priest may be duty bound to warn or remonstrate with the Bishop. It is no act of insubordination if a subject warns, or even remonstrates with his superior, who by forgetfulness of his office is endangering the important interests of the Church. An appropriate example of this is contained in the incident at Antioch, where St. Paul withstood St. Peter to the face. Galatians, 2, 11-21.

"Christianity," as Scherer (1845-1918) pointed out, "knows no absolute obedience, not even to the papacy . . . Canonical obedience is objectively limited: it is not a blind obedience, nor does it depend upon a subjective insight into the legitimacy of the command or upon the personal conviction of the intrinsic excellence of the command." [39]

By blind obedience is meant that obedience by which an inferior carries out every command of his superior without making any inquiry into the matter commanded.[40] Such an obedience is truly blind and irrational, for obedience is a matter of the will, which normally does not operate independently of the intellect. On the contrary, the will is dependent upon the intellect.

(39) Das Christenthum kennt keinen absoluten Gehorsam, auch nicht gegenüber dem Papste . . . Die kanonische Obedienz ist demnach eine objectiv beschränkte, einerseits kein blinder Gehorsam, aber anderseits auch nicht von der Einsicht in die innere Rechtsmässigkeit und von der Ueberzeugung der Vortrefflichkeit des Mandatsbedingt.—*Scherer, Handbuch des Kirchenrechts* (2 vols., Graz, 1886-1898), I, 444.

(40) Ascetical and spiritual writers use this term, "blind obedience," in many different senses, but practically always they use it in a sense different from the one in which it is used in this work. For a detailed study of the use of the term employed by ascetical writers cf. Raus, *De Sacrae Obedientiae Virtute et Voto*, pp. 49-64.

Canonical obedience, as was seen in the preceding article, is definitely determined as to its object. Hence a cleric has a perfect right to inquire whether the given command is within or outside the jurisdiction of the Bishop. In canonical obedience there is not demanded a conformity of the speculative judgment on the part of the cleric to the mind of the Bishop. Canonical obedience does, however, demand the conformity of the practical judgment to the order given. The command materially considered in itself may, at times, be imprudent or inopportune; but obedience to it does not imply an approval of it as such on the part of one's speculative judgment.[41]

The promise of obedience obliges a secular cleric to nothing more than the material execution of the command. A secular cleric does not incur the obligation of obedience which a Religious assumes in conjunction with the vow of obedience, and accordingly he has no obligation of striving to conform his mind to that of the Bishop. Any morally good motive, even that of fulfilling his promise of obedience, suffices.

Canonical obedience should be prompt, i.e., it should be carried out in accord with the time limit contained in the command, e.g. immediately, as soon as possible, within one month, within a year, etc.

Furthermore, canonical obedience should be integral, i.e., exactly in accord with the principles of the interpretation of law (canons 17-21), and without cavil concerning the interpretation of the words.

(41) Raus, *De Sacrae Obedientiae Virtute et Voto*, p. 54.

EPILOGUE

One of the most humane canons in the Code of Canon Law is canon 2214, §2, which is taken verbatim from the 13th Session, *de ref.*, chapter 1, of the Council of Trent:

"Bishops and other Ordinaries should remember that they are shepherds and not slave-drivers, and that they must so rule over their subjects as not to domineer over them but to love them as sons and brothers; they should endeavor by exhortation and admonition to deter them from wrongdoing lest they be obliged to administer due punishment after faults have been committed. Yet if through human frailty their subjects do wrong, they must observe the precept of the Apostle, and reprove, entreat, rebuke them in all patience and doctrine; for sympathy is often more effective for correction than severity, exhortation better than threats of punishment, kindness better than insistence on authority. If in view of the seriousness of a crime there be need of punishment, they must combine authority with leniency, judgment with mercy, severity with moderation, to the end that discipline, so salutary and essential to public order, be maintained without asperity, and that those who have been punished may amend their ways, or, if they refuse to do so, that others may be deterred from wrongdoing by the salutary example of their punishment." [42]

A logical conclusion to be drawn from this canon, which outlines the attitude that should guide Bishops in the exercise of their jurisdiction, is that clerics have the corresponding duty to respect and obey their Bishops as their spiritual fathers or older brothers, from whom they may expect, from time to time, exhortations and admonitions. And if through the frailty of human nature they

[42] Canon 2214, 2. Translation from Bouscaren-Ellis, *Canon Law*, pp. 800-801.

do wrong, then they must expect and accept correction from their Shepherd.

Such should be the relationship existing between Bishop and clergy! Such was the mind of Pope Pius XI in his encyclical letter on the Catholic Priesthood, when he stated that, if such an ideal relationship existed, then the Church Militant would constitute a veritable army set in array.

"Let then obedience bind ever closer together the various members of the Hierarchy, one with another, and all with the Head; and thus make the Church Militant a foe truly terrible to the enemies of God, *ut castrorum aciem ordinatam,* as an army set in array. Let obedience temper excessive zeal on the one hand, and put the spur to weakness and slackness on the other. Let it assign to each his place and station. Let each accept without resistance. Otherwise the magnificent work of the Church in the world would be sadly hindered. Let each see in the arrangement of his hierarchical superiors the arrangements of the only true Head, whom all obey, Jesus Christ our Lord, who became for us 'obedient unto death, even to the death on the cross'." (43)

This obligation of obedience on the part of clerics, especially of priests, has been the object of solicitude of the presently gloriously reigning Supreme Pontiff, Pope Pius XII. In his Apostolic Exhortation of September 23, 1950, addressed to all the clergy of the entire world, the Holy Father, in commenting on the formation of the clergy, particularly of seminarians, has this to say concerning the obedience which is expected of them:

"It is necessary that young men acquire the spirit of obedience by accustoming themselves to submit their own will sincerely to that of God manifested through the legitimate authority of their superiors. . . From the

(43) Pius XI, litt encycl. *Ad catholici sacerdotii,* 20 dec. 1935, c. II—*AAS,* XXVIII (1935), 32.

seminary on, the future priest must learn to give filial and sincere obedience to his superiors in order to be always ready later on to obey his Bishop docilely."[44]

Obedience to the Church and her lawfully constituted authorities, the Holy Father points out, often demands great sacrifices on the part of priests. As in the days of the Apostles, so today, canonical obedience may even be the occasion of persecution and imprisonment.

"In an age like ours, in which the principle of authority is grievously disturbed, it is absolutely necessary that the priest, keeping the precepts of faith firmly in mind, should consider and duly accept this same authority, not only as the bulwark of the social and religious order, but also as the foundation of his own personal sanctification. While the enemies of God, with criminal astuteness, are trying to incite and solicit people's unruly passions, to make them rise up against the commands of Holy Mother Church, we wish to give due praise to, and animate with paternal encouragement, that vast army of ministers of God, who, in order to manifest openly their Christian obedience and to preserve intact their fidelity to Christ and to the legitimate authority established by Him, 'have been counted worthy to suffer disgrace for the name of Jesus,' and not only disgrace, but persecutions, imprisonment and even death."[45]

(44) Pius XII, adhortatio Apostolica, *Menti Nostrae,* 23 sept. 1950, *AAS,* XXXXII (1950), 662, N.C.W.C. Translation, Washington, D. C., p. 25.

(45) *AAS,* XXXXII (1950), 690; N.C.W.C. Translation, Washington, D. C., p. 8.

CONCLUSIONS

1. Canonical obedience has its origin in incardination, (pp. 62).

2. The promise of obedience made at ordination to the priesthood is merely an external enhancement of an already existing obligation, (p. 73).

3. The promise of obedience made by secular priests is different from the vow of obedience made by members of Religious Institutes, (p. 61).

4. Specific canonical obedience relates to all the commands of the Ordinary, even when these commands merely restate a law of the Code, a law of a particular Council, or a diocesan statute. These commands may take the form of a particular precept, (pp. 101-107).

5. Canonical obedience is not an absolute or a blind obedience, nor does it *per se* pertain to civil or personal matters, (pp. 116-118).

BIBLIOGRAPHY

Sources

Acta Apostolicae Sedis, Commentarium Officiale, Romae, 1909-1929; Civitate Vaticana, 1929—

Acta et Decreta Councilii Plenarii Baltimorensis III, A.D. *MDCCC-LXXXIV,* Baltimorae: John Murphy, 1886.

Acta et Decreta Sacrorum Conciliorum Recentiorum, Collectio Lacensis, 7 vols., Friburgi Brisgoviae, 1870-1892.

Bouscaren T. Lincoln, *The Canon Law Digest,* 2 vols. and Supplement through 1948, Milwaukee, Wis.: The Bruce Publishing Company, 1934-1943-1949.

Bruns, Hermann,*Canones Apostolorum et Conciliorum Saeculorum IV-VII,* 2 vols., Berolini, 1939.

Codex Iuris Canonici Pii X Pontificis Maximi iussu digestus, Benedicti Papae XV auctoritate promulgatus, Praefatione, Fontium Annotatione et Indice Analytico-Alphabetico ab Emo Petro Card. Gasparri Auctus, Romae, Typis Polyglottis Vaticanis, 1917; reimpressio, 1934.

Codicis Iuris Canonici Fontes, cura Emi Card. Gasparri editi, 9 vols., Romae (postea Civitate Vaticana): Typis Polyglottis Vaticanis, 1923-1939. (Vols. VII-IX, ed. cura et studio Emi. Iustiniani Card. Serédi).

Collectanea in usum Secretariae Sacrae Congregationis Episcoporum et Regularium, 2. ed., ed. A. Bizzarri, Romae, 1885.

Collectanea S. Congregationis de Propaganda Fide, 2 vols., Romae: Typographia Polyglotta S.C. de Propaganda Fide, 1907.

Concilii Plenarii Baltimorensis II, in Ecclesia Metropolitana Baltimorensi, a die VII ad diem XXI Octobris, A.D. MDCCCLXVI, Habiti et a Sede Apostolica Recogniti, Acta et Decreta, Baltimorae, John Murphy, 1868.

Concilia Provincialia Baltimori Habita ab anno 1829 *usque ad annum* 1849, ed. altera, Baltimori, John Murphy, 1851.

Corpus Iuris Canonici, ed. Lipsiensis secunda, post Aemilii Richteri curas . . . instruxit Aemilius Friedberg, 2 vols., Lipsiae, 1879-1881.

Decretales D. Gregorii Papae IX, suae integritati una cum glossis restitutae, cum privilegio Gregorii XIII, Pont. Max., et Aliorum Principum, Romae, 1582.

Decretum Gratiani emendatum et notationibus illustratum una cum glossis, Gregorii XIII, Pont. Max., iussu editum, 2 vols., Romae, 1582.

Duchesne, Louis, *Le Liber Pontificales,* 2 vols., Paris, 1886-1892.

Hardouin, Jean, *Acta Conciliorum et Episcolae Decretales ac Constitutiones, Summorum Pontificum,* 12 vols., Parisiis, 1714-1715.

Hartzheim, Joseph, *Concilia Germaniae,* 10 vols., Coloniae Augustae Agrippensium, 1759-1790.

Jaffé, Philippus, *Regesta Pontificum Romanorum ab condita Ecclesia ad annum post Christum natum MCXCVIII,* ed. correctam et auctam auspiciis Gulielmi Wattenbach curaverunt S. Löwenfeld, F. Kaltenbrunner, P. Ewald, 2 vols., Lipsiae, 1885-1888.

Mansi, Joannes, *Sacrorum Conciliorum Nova et Amplissima Collectio,* 53 vols. in 60, Parisiis, 1901-1927.

Monumenta Germaniae Historica, Legum Sectio II, *Capitularia,* Tomus I, *Capitularia Regum Francorum,* denuo edidit Alfredus Boretius, Hannoverae, 1888.

——————— Legum Sectio III, *Concilia,* Tomus I, *Concilia Aevi Merovingici,* recensuit Fridericus Maassen, Hannoverae, 1883.

Pontificale Romanum in tres partes distributum, ed., Joseph Catalanus, 3 vols., Parisiis, 1850.

Potthast, Augustus, *Regesta Pontificus Romanorum inde ab anno post Christum natum MCXCVIII ad annum MCCCIV,* 2 vols., Berolini, 1874-1875.

Schroeder, Henry J., *Canons and Decrees of the Council of Trent,* St. Louis: B. Herder Book Co., 1941.

REFERENCE WORKS

Amort, Eusebius, *Elementa Iuris Canonici Veteris et Moderni,* 3 vols., Ferrariae, 1763.

Augustine, Charles, *A Commentary on the New Code of Canon Law,* 3. ed., 8 vols., St. Louis; Herder, 1918-1931.

——————— *Rights and Duties of Ordinaries,* St. Louis; Herder, 1924.

Baldus de Ubaldis, *Super Decretalibus,* Lugduni, 1547.

Barbosa, Augustinus, *Collectanea Doctorum tam Veterum quam Recentiorum in Ius Pontificium Universum,* 6 vols., Lugduni, 1656.

Berutti, Christophorus, *Institutiones Iuris Canonici,* 5 vols., Taurini-Romae: Marietti, 1936-1943.

Beste, Udalricus, *Introductio in Codicem,* 2. ed., Collegeville, Minnesota: St. John's Abbey Press, 1946.

Blat, Albertus, *Commentarium Textus Codicis Iuris Canonici,* 5 vols. in 6, Romae, 1919-1927; Liber II, *De Religiosis.*

Boich, Henricus, *Commentaria in Quinque Decretalium Libros,* Venetiis, 1576.

Bouix, D., *Tractatus de Episcopo,* 2 vols., Parisiis, 1859.

Bouscaren, T. L.,-Ellis, Adam C., *Canon Law,* Milwaukee, Wisconsin: Bruce Publishing Co., 1946.

Cappello, Felix, *Summa Iuris Canonici,* 3 vols., Vol. I and II, 4. ed., 1945; Vol. III, 3. ed., 1948 Romae: Apud Aedes Universitatis Gregorianae.

Chelodi, Joannes, *Ius de Personis,* 2. ed., Tridenti: Libr. Edit. Tridentum, 1927.

Cicognani, Amleto, *Canon Law,* 2. ed., The Dolphin Press, Philadelphia, 1935.

Claeys-Bouúaert, Ferdinandus, *De Canonica Cleri Saecularis Obedientia,* Lovanii, 1904.

Clancy, Patrick, *The Local Religious Superior,* The Catholic University of America Canon Law Studies, n. 175, Washington, D. C.: The Catholic University of America Press, 1943.

Coronata, Mattheus Conte a, *Institutiones Iuris Canonici,* 4 vols., Taurini: Marietti, 1928-1935.

De Luca, Joannes Card., *Theatrum Veritatis et Justitiae,* 16 vols., Coloniae Agrippinae, 1706.

Donnelly, Francis, *The Diocesan Synod,* The Catholic University of America Canon Law Studies, n. 74, Washington, D. C.: The Catholic University of America, 1932.

Donovan, John Thomas, *The Clerical Obligations of Canon* 138 *and* 140, The Catholic University of America Canon Law Studies, n. 272, Washington, D. C.: The Catholic University of America Press, 1948.

Fagnanus, Prosperus, *Commentaria in Quinque Libros Decretalium,* 5 vols., Romae, 1661.

Fanfani, Ludovicus, I., *De Iure Religiosorum ad Normam Codicis Iuris Canonici,* 2. ed., Taurini-Romae: Ex officia Libraria Marietti, 1925.

Gonzalez-Tellez, Emmanuel, *Commentaria Perpetua in Singulos Quinque Librorum Decretalium Gregorii IX,* 5 vols., Lugduni, 1673.

Guido de Baiso, *Rosarium, seu In Decretalium Volumen Commentaria,* Venetiis,

Hallier, Franciscus, *De Sacris Electionibus et Ordinationibus,* 2. ed., 3 vols., Romae, 1740.

Haring, Johann B., *Grundzüge des katholischen Kirchenrechts,* 3. ed., 2 vols., Graz, Moser, 1924.

Hinschius, Paulus, *Decretales Pseudo Isidorianae et Capitula Angilramni* Lipsiae, 1863.

——————— *Das Kirchenrecht der Katholiken und Protestanten in Deutschland,* 6 vols., Berlin, 1869-1897.

Hostiensis, Cardinalis (Henricus de Segusio), *Commentaria in Quinque Decretalium Libros,* 5 vols., Venetiis, 1581.

Jone, Heribertus, *Commentarium in Codicem Iuris Canonici,* Vol. I, Paderborn: F. Schöningh, 1950-1952.

Leitner, Martin, *Handbuch des katholischen Kirchenrechts,* 5 vols., Vol. III, *Das Ordensrecht,* 2. ed., 1922, Regensburg: Kösel und Pustet, 1919-1927.

Leurenius, Petrus, *Ius Canonicum Universum,* 5 vols. in 4, Venetiis, 1729.

McBride, James, *Incardination and Excardination of Seculars,* The Catholic University of America Canon Law Studies, n. 145, Washington, D. C., 1941.

McClunn, Justin, *Administrative Recourse,* The Catholic University of America Canon Law Studies, n. 240, Washington, D. C.: The Catholic University of America Press, Washington, D. C., 1946.

Martène, Edmundus, *De Antiquis Ecclesiae Ritibus,* 2. ed., 4 vols., Antverpii, 1736-1737.

Michaels, Gommarus, *Normae Generales Iuris Canonici,* 2 vols., Lublin: Universitas Catholica, 1929.

Migne, Jacques Paul, *Patrologiae Cursus Completus, Series Graeca,* 161 vols., Parisiis, 1857-1866.

——————— *Patrologiae Cursus Completus, Series Latina,* 221 vols., Parisiis, 1844-1864.

Muratori, Ludovicus, *Antiquitates Italicae Medii Aevii,* 6 vols., Mediolani, 1738-1843.

Noldin, Hieronymus-Schmitt, A., *Summa Theologiae Moralis,* 3 vols., Vol. II, 27. ed., Oeniponte: Typis et Sumptibus Fel. Rauch, 1950.

Ojetti, B., *Commentarium in Codicem Iuris Canonici,* 4 vols., Romae: Apud Aedes Universitatis Gregorianae, 1927-1931.

O'Neill, Francis, *The Dismissal of Religious in Temporary Vows,* The Catholic University of America Canon Law Studies, n. 166, Washington, D. C.: The Catholic University of America Press, 1942.

Panormitanus, Abbas (Nicholaus de Tudeschis), *Commentaria in Quinque Libros Decretalium,* 5 vols. in 7, Venetiis, 1588.

Phillips, Georg, *Kirchenrecht,* 2. ed., 7 vols., Regensburg, 1845-1872.

Pichler, Vitus, *Candidatus Iurisprudentiae Sacrae,* 4. ed., 5 vols., Ingolstadii, 1724-1728.

Pirhing, Ernicus, *Ius Canonicum, Nova Methodo Explicatum, Omnibus Capitulis* Titulorum, 5 vols. in 3, Dilingae, 1722.

Prümmer, Dominicus, *Manuale Iuris Canonici,* 3. ed., Friburgi Brisgoviae: Herder, 1928.

Ramstein, Matthew, *A Manual of Canon Law,* Hoboken, New Jersey, Terminal Printing and Publishing Co., 1948.

Raus, J. B., *De Sacrae Obedientiae Virtute et Voto,* Lugduni, 1923.

Reiffenstuel, Anacletus, *Ius Canonicum Universum,* 5 vols. in 7, Parisiis, 1864-1870.

Richter, Aemilius-Dove, Richard, *Kirchenrecht,* 8. ed., 2 vols., Leipzig, 1886.

Roberti, F., *De Delictis et Poenis,* ed. altera, Romae: Libraria Pontificii Instituti Utriusque Iuris, 1938.

Rufinus, *Summa Decretorum,* ed. Heinrich Singer, Paderborn, 1902.

Ryan, Gerald, *Principles of Episcopal Jurisdiction,* The Catholic University of America Canon Law Studies, n. 120, Washington, D. C.: The Catholic University of America Press, 1939.

Schaefer, Timotheus, *De Religiosis ad Normam Codicis Iuris Canonici,* 3. ed., Romae, 1940.

Scherer, Rudolph Ritter von, *Handbuch des Kirchenrechts,* 2 vols., Graz, 1886-1898.

Schmalzgrueber, Franciscus, *Ius Ecclesiasticum Universum,* 5 vols. in 12, Romae, 1843.

Schneider, Edelhard Louis, *Status of Secularized Ex-Religious Clerics,* The Catholic University of America Canon Law Studies, n. 284, Washington, D. C.: The Catholic University of America Press, 1948.

Schroeder, Henry J., *Disciplinary Decrees of the General Councils,* St. Louis: B. Herder Book Co., 1937.

Schulte, Johann Friedrich, *System des allgemeinen katholischen Kirchenrechts,* Giessen, 1856.

Sweeney, Francis, *The Reduction of Clerics to the Lay State,* The Catholic University of America Canon Law Studies, n. 223, Washington, D. C.: The Catholic University of America Press, 1945.

Thomassinus, Ludovicus, *Vetus et Nova Ecclesiae Disciplina circa Beneficia et Beneficiarios,* 10 vols., Moguntiaci, 1787.

Toso, Albertus, *Ad Codicem Iuris Canonici . . . Commentaria Minora,* 5 vols. in 2, Taurini-Romae, 1920-1927.

Vermeersch, Arthurus-Creusen, Josephus, *Epitome Iuris Canonici,* 3 vols., Vol. I, 7. ed., 1949; Vol. II, 6. ed., 1940; Vol. III, 6. ed., 1946; Mechlinae-Romae: H. Dessain.

Wernz, F. X.-Vidal, P., *Ius Canonicum,* 7 vols. in 8, Vol. I, 2. ed., 1951; Vol. VII, 1937; Romae: Apud Aedes Universitatis Gregorianae.

Woywod, Stanislaus, *A Practical Commentary on the Code of Canon Law,* revised by Callistus Smith, revised and enlarged edition, 2 vols., New York: Jos. F. Wagner, Inc., 1948.

ARTICLES

Chapman, John, "Cornelius," *The Catholic Encyclopedia,* IV, 375-376.

——————— "Novatian and Novatianism," *The Catholic Encyclopedia,* XI, 138-141.

Kuttner, Stephan, "The Father of the Science of Canon Law," *The Jurist,* 1941, 2-9.

Schaaf, Valentine, "Episcopus proprius ordinationis religiosorum," *The Ecclesiastical Review,* XC (1934), 491-509.

Schneider, Ph., "Der Kanonische Gehorsam," *Archiv für katholisches Kirchenrecht,* LXXXII (1902), 290-324.

PERIODICALS

Archiv für katholisches Kirchenrecht, Innsbruck, 1857-1861; Mainz, 1862-

Ecclesiastical Review, The (originally, *The American Ecclesiastical Review*), Philadelphia, 1889-

Jurist, The, Washington, D. C., 1941-

LIST OF ABBREVIATIONS

AAS—*Acta Apostolicae Sedis.*

Amort—*Elementa Iuris Canonici Veteris et Moderni.*

Bruns—*Canones Apostolorum et Conciliorum Saeculorum IV-VII.*

Coll. Lac.—*Acta et Decreta Sacrorum Conciliorum Recentiorum, Collectio Lacensis.*

Digest—*The Canon Law Digest.*

Fontes—*Codicis Iuris Canonici Fontes.*

Hardouin—*Conciliorum Collectio Regia Maxima.*

Jaffé—*Regesta Pontificum Romanorum.*

Leurenius—*Ius Canonicum Universum.*

Mansi—*Sacrorum Conciliorum Nova et Amplissima Collectio.*

MGH—*Monumenta Germaniae Historica.*

MPG—Migne, *Patrologia Series Graeca.*

MPL—Migne, *Patrologia Series Latina.*

Muratori—*Antiquitates Italicae Medii Aevii.*

Noldin—Noldin-Schmitt, *Summa Theologiae Moralis.*

Pichler—*Candidatus Iurisprudentiae Sacrae.*

Pirhing—*Ius Canonicum in Quinque Libros Decretalium.*

Reiffenstuel—*Ius Canonicum Universum.*

Schmalzgrueber—*Ius Ecclesiasticum Universum.*

Thomassinus—*Vetus et Nova Ecclesiae Disciplina circa Beneficia et Beneficiarios.*

Wernz-Vidal—*Ius Canonicum ad Codicis Norman Exactum.*

ALPHABETICAL INDEX

BIOGRAPHICAL NOTE

Joseph George Sheehan was born on August 16, 1917, at Stewartville, Minnesota. He received his primary education at Blessed Sacrament School, Seattle, Washington, and St. Mary's Catholic School, Bird Island, Minnesota. He graduated from St. Paul's Mission House, Epworth, Iowa, in June, 1935, and from Sacred Heart College, Girard, Pennsylvania, in June 1937.

He completed his theological studies at the St. Paul Seminary, St. Paul, Minnesota, and was ordained to the priesthood on October 29, 1944. His first appointment was that of Chancellor of the Diocese of Crookston, Crookston, Minnesota.

On October 3, 1950, he enrolled in the School of Canon Law at the Catholic University of America, Washington, D. C. He received the degree of Baccalaureate in Canon Law in June 1951, and the degree of Licentiate in Canon Law in June, 1952.

CANON LAW STUDIES*

337. Bourque, Rev. John R., S.T.L., J.C.L., The Judicial Power of the Church—Canon 1553, §1.

338. Cornell, Rev. Charles E., A.B., S.T.B., J.C.L., The Juridical Status of Heretics and Schismatics in Good Faith.

339. Fitzgerald, Rev. William Francis, A.B., S.T.L., J.C.L., The Parish Census and the *Liber Status Animarum*.

340. Kubik, Rev. Stanislaus J., S.T.D., J.C.L., Invalidity of Dispensations according to canon 84, §1.

341. Nugent, Rev. John Gerard, C.M., J.C.L., Ordination in Societies of the Common Life.

342. Peterson, Rev. Casimir Melvyn, S.S., A.B., S.T.L., J.C.L., Spiritual Care in Diocesan Seminaries.

343. Reiss, Rev. John Charles, A.B., S.T.L., J.C.L., The Time and Place of Sacred Ordination.

344. Sheehan, Rev. Joseph George, J.C.L., The Obligation of Respect and Obedience of Clerics to their Ordinary—Canon 127.

345. Shekleton, Rev. Matthew M., O.S.M., J.C.L., Doctrinal Interpretation of Law.

346. Viau, Rev. Roger, S.T.L., J.C.L., Doubt in Canon Law.

347. Walsh, Rev. Donnell Anthony, A.B., J.C.L., The New Law on Secular Institutes.

348. Sesto, Rev. Gennaro Joseph, S.D.B., A.B., S.T.L., J.C.L., Guardians of the Mentally Ill in Ecclesiastical Trials.

349. Fus, Rev. Edward A., A.B., J.C.L., The Extraordinary Form of Marriage According to Canon 1098.

* For a complete list of the available numbers of this series apply to the Catholic University of America Press, 620 Michigan Avenue, N.E., Washington (17), D. C.

www.ingramcontent.com/pod-product-compliance
Lightning Source LLC
LaVergne TN
LVHW050210080826
844660LV00012B/392

* 9 7 8 0 8 1 3 2 2 5 1 2 8 *